POETRY OF
Spiritual Awakening

POETRY OF Spiritual Awakening

reflections of awareness

HILTON L. ANDERSON

iUniverse, Inc.
Bloomington

Poetry of Spiritual Awakening
Reflections of Awareness

iUniverse books may be ordered through booksellers or by contacting:

iUniverse
1663 Liberty Drive
Bloomington, IN 47403
www.iuniverse.com
1-800-Authors (1-800-288-4677)

ISBN: 978-1-4620-5655-2 (sc)
ISBN: 978-1-4620-5657-6 (hc)
ISBN: 978-1-4620-5656-9 (e)

Printed in the United States of America

iUniverse rev. date: 10/13/2011

Contents

External Awareness

Waking Up

Awake

Teachers

We are all simultaneously teachers and learners.
We teach what we believe and learn from the beliefs of others.
Teach from the highest awareness of Self.
Share the truth as you best understand it,
Because that is who you are.

Introduction

Poetry is wonderful shorthand for expressing your ideas and beliefs. It is compressed complexity. It is complexity expressed as we understand it in a given moment. The process of change in consciousness is not just reflected in the poetry; the writing of the poetry itself is part of the process of awakening or changing. Poetry allows one to realize in a succinct way where one's thinking is at each point in development. Poetry is an expression of both the rational and the intuitive in a concise form that helps lead to expanded awareness.

The poetry in this book should not be judged from a literary perspective but rather from the perspective of the ideas conveyed in the poems. Most of the poems are expressions of philosophical, psychological, or religious concepts dealing with my evolving understanding of the nature of existence and self.

My first poems grew out of the frustration and the boredom of a meaningless job in the insurance industry, my first job after graduating from undergraduate college. I came to believe that the insurance industry, like the navy as described in the book the *Caine Mutiny,* was designed by geniuses but administered by idiots. (See my poems "Time for a Change" and "Status Quo.") These poems, in addition to the simple expression of frustration, were an outgrowth of a desperate search for meaning and self-worth through self-expression, since there was no opportunity to do so at work. These early poems took various forms but never transcended the ego level of awareness.

Later in life, my poetry became my way of trying to express what I was learning about myself and the world around me. My poetry evolved into the expression of my spiritual development as my search for meaning expanded. There were many events that prompted this interest in the spiritual, but none more powerful than my confrontation of my mother's death. (See my poem "Death Watch.")

Despite my professional training as a psychologist and my working as a school psychologist for twenty-five years, I realized that I understood little about the meaning of death. Many of the medical professionals in the hospital at the time of her death seemed to deny or were unable to deal with discussing her approaching death with the family. This caused me to wonder about the adequacy of science in understanding this important, life-changing event. This experience began my sustained journey of spiritual inquiry.

You will probably notice that death holds a prominent position in my poetry. Death is a powerful teacher for all of us. Particular poems represent important turning points in my journey through life. The first of these pivotal poems is "Firstborn." My wife and I had difficulty having children, and after great effort, she conceived and carried our baby to full term, only to have him stillborn. This event opened an awareness in me of the suffering of others, as many people shared their experience of having an unsuccessful pregnancy. It was an early lesson that life is suffering, as taught by Buddha in the story of the mustard seed.

My response to this event was initially purely at the ego level, making alterations in the external world. I changed jobs, went to graduate school, and changed professions. It became manifestly obvious that death could not be avoided and that I had very little, if any, understanding of it.

Another major event was my developing a melanoma, and my personal experience is depicted in my poem "The Healing." Spiritual development is still very much a work in progress, despite my age and the passage of many years. It is, I believe, the essential task of life. It is why we are here. Some people never awaken to this spiritual need and are content to remain at their ego level, believing that external reality is all that matters.

It should be pointed out that the development of awareness is not a linear event. There are jumps and starts, regressions and plateaus as awareness unfolds, as expressed in my poem "The Spiral Staircase." Poems in this book are arranged into three broad categories of evolving awareness. The first is external awareness. The second is waking up, or the beginning of the development of internal awareness. The third consists of those poems that best express my current state of spiritual understanding.

In *A Search for the Source,* I suggest that humanity's spiritual awareness may be categorized into three levels of awareness, as depicted in my poem "Asleep Awake Enlightened." The vast majority of people are asleep; that is, they are unaware of their own spiritual reality. A significant number are waking up to their spiritual reality, while very few are actually spiritually enlightened.

"External Awareness" falls into the category of sleeping, because the orientation is toward the external world, with perhaps various levels of sensitivity but mostly devoid of recognition of a spiritual reality. The second category of internal awareness is labeled "Waking Up, because it is the beginning of becoming aware of spirit, unseen and unheard, yet present. My present state of awareness, the third category, I would describe as a somewhat more advanced state of awakening, thus labeled "awake," but short of enlightenment.

Some of the poems in this book have been published in my two previous books, *A Search for the Source* and *Peace Is Oneness.* But this is the first time that I am attempting to present my poetry in a form that reflects my developing awareness. This development only became apparent to me in retrospect, and my ability to arrange my poetry into some coherent and meaningful order has only now become possible. Whether this order, meaningful to me, is meaningful and useful to the reader, only you can tell. Clearly, these three sections are somewhat arbitrary. The assignment of poems to each category is my personal choice, with which others may legitimately disagree.

A Course in Miracles, a contemporary Gnostic Gospel, was, and is, a powerful source of spiritual inspiration and understanding, and its concepts are expressed in much of my poetry. My study of "the course" over many years is reflected in the changing beliefs expressed in my poems.

I don't consider myself enlightened and, therefore, am not able to provide poetry descriptive of that state of being. Second, and more fundamentally, that state of spiritual enlightenment does not lend itself to expression in language. Language can take us only so far. Enlightenment is a condition of awareness that can only be experienced and is, therefore, difficult to share with others unless they, too, have a similar experience. Mystical religions, depth psychology, and many other methods are designed to help people have experiences of enlightenment. Enlightenment can only be hinted at in language.

A test you may wish to apply to yourself is to consider which poems you like the most. If they cluster in one of the three groups of poems, you might reasonably conclude that this area represents your present level of awareness, interest, and spiritual development

Become aware of those poems you strongly disagree with or you feel are simply wrong or make you feel uncomfortable. These represent spiritual sticking points: either yours or mine. Spiritual awakening is a process of realizing that the Divine Plan is a perfect creation, because it is based on universal love. Everything is already perfect at the spiritual level, and if you perceive it otherwise, it is an error or misperception on your part or mine, stemming from our separated ego state. It represents creation not in harmony with universal love, the Divine Plan. It is yours or my spiritual growth point.

The purpose of writing this book is the hope that my poems will be helpful to others in their unfolding spiritual journey. We are all on the same spiritual path, although each path appears unique to each individual. Your path is your only means to your own spiritual awareness. Have fun and enjoy. I hope this will be helpful. Remember: don't just read with your rational mind. Be open to your intuitive sense, your heart. To make spiritual progress, we need both the rational and the intuitive. Remember that in this society, the rational is dominant, so you need to make a special effort to involve your intuitive knowing.

External Awareness

The Status Quo

Slowly, slowly, ever so slowly the clock moves; or is it moving?
The stretch of time exalts the pain of drudgery and boredom.
The boss explains there's too much hair, not enough despair.
In twenty years a bulbous pot proclaims
The change that only time has wrought.
Annually a new assault is brought with each June's graduation.
Like waves upon a rocky shore, the great roar
Leaves more unchanged than altered.
Endless time, seconds, minutes, hours, days,
And what has changed? The boss is gone!
But oh, subtle time, a new boss you've wrought,
Thin hair, protruding waist, proclaimer of the status quo.

Time for a Change

The endless, ceaseless drift of days,
The monotonous drudgery of insignificant tasks,
The stagnate hopelessness of mundane work,
The crass and callus grasp for gold,
The philosophic hollowness of stunting materialism:
Oh, for a glimpse of meaning, a feeling of self-worth,
A pride in doing, of being, of knowing
That one's life is of value somehow.

Work

Someday my work here will be done.
Today, tomorrow, its conclusion will come.
Its purpose at times clearly seen,
At others, obscured beyond human ken,
Relevant often only to one's self-esteem.

The larger plan unknown to man is
A conclusion that humility demands.
Far-reaching effects of simple deeds,
Little consequence of others the world often heeds.
In the end, what judgment as life recedes?

There is a knowing deep within
That in the end only love extends.
The truth is that work is love expressed,
Its fruits reflect what each intends,
The betterment of all, its fulfilling end.

Childhood Remembered

Got a cut here on my arm,
It's still bleeding, but no harm.
Got this gash on my knee
Climbing up an apple tree.
Bent a fender, broke two spokes,
Gave the handlebar a dent.
You can fix it for a few cents.
Tore my seat on a barbed wire fence.
Lost my penknife, no defense;
Holes in pockets make no sense.
Darnedest fall I ever took
Was crossing a little brook,
Slipping on a stone that shook.

Swimming down in old Green Brook,
How did mother know?
She never peeked a look.
Making model planes all day;
How they flew, I'd rather not say.
Marbles was the game in town,
Occupying every boy around.
Kept mother busy mending knees
In every pair of pants she'd see.
Halloween was a favorite time,
Trick or treat, mask and mime.
Cavities, never mind:
My favorite candy was lime.

The sled and skates were always out
From December 'til crocus sprout.
There never was enough snow
To keep children happy, you know.
Although one winter I recall
The snow seemed almost ten feet tall.
Most of us began to think
That we had begun to shrink.
My grandma used to worry a lot,
When I was just a little tot.
That failure might be my eventual lot.
But this I never managed to do
Until I was well past twenty-two.

What Bends the Twig?

As the twig is bent so grows the tree.
But what bends the twig?
Material science says
Heredity and environment.
Religion says
Reincarnation and karma.
As ye sow so shall ye reap.
Clearly heredity has a profound effect.
Did we choose our heredity,
As karma and reincarnation imply?
Early environment has
Significant, long-lasting effects.
Is birth into a particular environment
An accident, a chance event,
Or is there some hidden cause?
Does life have a spiritual plan,
Or is physical materiality all there is,
With chaos theory at its source?
Must science and religion
Forever be at odds,
Or are they different views
Of the same reality
That can be reconciled?

Dawn's Voice

Bird songs before daylight swell,
Sunrise their chorus foretells.
Every day greeted in the zeal,
Of their joyous vocal appeal.

This greeting of the rising sun
Triggers feelings that deeply run,
Touching something at the very core,
Life force released in every song.

Renewal not just for today,
But of endless dawn songs yet to play.
Reassurance that life is here again,
Following winter's silent stay.

Summer Morning

The morning mist slowly melts away,
Near shore revealed, later trees across the lake.
Clouds still obscure mountaintops beyond the shore.
Soft reflections harden as the mist drifts off.
Wind rustles nearby leaves,
Ripple patterns form off shore,
Enlarge, soon the mirror is gone.
Bright light breaks out everywhere.
Hot summer sun's day begun.
Morning's magic awaits another dawn.

The Lake on a Summer Night

Not a ripple disturbs the glassy lake.
Surface ablaze with star reflections make
The night sky's dual image seem
A vision in a wondrous dream.

From shore to shore the frogs ignore
The stillness with their hoarse croaks.
A prelude to the loon's magic call,
Soon to be silenced by the coming fall.

Mother Black Duck sleeps with her new brood,
Disturbed by others, stalking their evening food.
The silent stars, time beacons, coldly shine,
Blinking in the firmament, uncaring, blind.

Continuity

The slab-log camp was rough, hand built
By a man known to others but not to me.
He knew which way the cool summer winds blow.
He found a spot upon the shore,
Where decades later the cabin endures.

"Maine is kind to wood," an old man said.
The proof confirmed in ancient structures
Abundant in towns along the coast,
Century-old houses from the past,
Weather-beaten, neglected, yet they last.

This legacy is taken for granted.
Easily forgotten, this timeless gift
From those who touch us from beyond.
Skilled work performed by past generations,
Love enshrined in wood for everyone's admiration.

The Rocking Chair

How many have sat here before?
Generation after generation,
Spiraling backward into the past.
How many more yet to come
Will know the comfort of this seat,
Moving in rhythmic gentle arcs,
As rounded rockers creep across the floor.
Son, daughter, grandmother, grandson,
Some on laps, some with dolls,
Rocking gently, feet on the floor,
Others careening, wildly not touching at all.
The cat and dog disdain the ride
And choose instead the sunlit rug.

To rock before the hearth in winter's cold,
On shaded porch in summer's heat,
In baby's room at feeding time,
Rocking a soothing lullaby.
What genius of design
Divined this evolution
Of motion from its static form,
Giving pleasure to all those
Who love the rhythm and the feel.
The gentle flow of time
Measured in each rocking creak,
Relaxing in the metered now.

The Nor'easter

Like a giant organ pipe, the fireplace flue
gives moaning voice to the gale's debut.
Across the roof, wind-driven rain
soon adds an erratic, tattooed refrain.
The slanting rain streaks salt-encrusted window panes,
transforming the world into an impressionist's view.
Window shades move to and fro in
response to each gust's heavy blow.
Wind-whipped dune grasses beckon gray cloud wisps
to shadow dance across rippled sand like phantom ships.
Blue-green colors ply mountainous waves,
each undulation enhanced.
Whitecaps stand atop moving crests;
frothy wisps blow in the air like snow.
Each breaker announced by a thundering roar,
a ceaseless, pulsing din.
Weary gulls dive and whirl,
then stand against the wind.
Driftwood, seaweed, shells, and froth ascend
to form a skirmish line across the beach.
High-water mark in this eternal plan
of changing wave and sculptured sand.

The Harbor

River and sea entwine
Where tug with barge combine,
And freighter and liner dock.

Where piers jut out and trucks pull in.
Amidst the whistles' shrilling din,
Cranes trace cargo arches overhead.

Barges filled with railroad cars make
Crisscross patterns as their wakes
Cross the courses ferries take.

Creosote infests the salted air,
Inspiring dreams of tall ships
That left this place without a trace.

The City

The jagged outline of the concrete mountain
Thrusts its symmetry above the bustling street.
Anodized metal quilts tinted glass facades.
Across the shadowed canyon's gulf
The prismatic mirror of the glazer's art
Reflects like a checkered mountain lake.

A mechanical roar echoes from the vertical gorge,
Where traffic streams flow in endless courses.
Taxi wheels hiss above the subway's rumble,
Marques glisten on the wet macadam,
Lights blinking without a sound.

On penthouse peaks ice cube clinks
Punctuate the conversant air.
Moneymen and thespians sit in adjacent chairs.
In an east side slum an alcoholic bum
Claws at the wall in fright,
From his achromatic show there is no flight.

The Parade

Around the corner, down the street,
The first cadenced beat is heard.
Then the clarion trumpet's call
Informs us all the band is near.
Can anything stir the marshal soul
Like a band in full array?
The bass drum's boom, the staccato snare,
The lines so straight in rhythm move.
The tuba's supporting base
Give slide trombones a place to glide.
Clarinets in high, rapid shrills
Add their lyrical rhythmic trills.
Baritone horns and saxophones
Support flutes and piccolos.
We raise our feet in cadence step
On the curb each march in place.
Being strong of will we don't step out
To join in Sousa's
"Stars and Stripes Forever" call.
But where is the call to peace,
That quiet melody to stir the soul
To love instead of hate?
Would Sousa now write that needed song
If he weren't already dead?
Would we respond or do we heed
Only the trumpet's strident call?

War's Ideology

Every war is a religious battle,
Because the brotherhood of man is shattered.
Separate and apart each fight,
Death's horrible specter always in sight.

Each judges the other to be an enemy.
Each side's grievances trumpeted by many,
Until each for the other feels only hate,
Aggression erupting in the name of the state.

War fosters the illusion that might makes right.
Each side entrapped by ideologies for which they fight.
The protagonists attempt to impose their will on each other.
Forgetting the knowledge they are each the other's brother.

War Is Hell

War is hell conceived in the minds of men.
Made manifest in the world as fears,
Religious, racial, tribal, political, cultural, economic,
A bottomless pit of unreconciled differences,
To be solved by force.
The killing begins,
Might makes right,
The wheel of aggression continues turning,
Endlessly creating anew
Fear anger and resentment.
Unity of creation unrecognized
As the single source of all.
The love, joy, and peace displaced,
Temporarily lost.
The choice is ours,
Belief in Heaven or hell.
Our answer is the world we create.

The Eve of a New Millennium

Two thousand years of war and strife,
The lesson taught but still unlearned.
How often will it repeat?
How much longer will it take?
Fears of loss, scarcity, and death
Take control of our lives.
Brotherhood lost in rivalry and competition.
Winning and losing the game of life.
The unlearned lesson so simple,
Yet so hard to grasp.
All worldly experiences
Seem to contradict it.
How could it be right?
At some level of being
The truth is known.
Love, abundance, and brotherhood
The foundation of eternal creation.
Know this truth.
It will set us free
In the Peace and Joy
We were born to be.

The Three Women of Maui

Granddaughter, grandmother, and daughter
Strolling along the beach
From water's edge up the sand
In line they stretched
From shortest to tallest
In harmony with the beach incline
From palm trees to water line,
But incorrect in generational order.
Almost a perfect trio in the morning sun.
Unaware of their harmony and disorder,
Just enjoying the day begun.

Of Trees and Men

Essential to the breath of life,
Replenisher of the air we breathe,
In quiet stillness stand, companion to the breeze,
Casting shadows where the daisies laze.

Giving voice to gusts
That announce the season's change,
Imperceptible rustle
In the evening solitude.

Fruitful sheltering arms upthrust
Against the sky silhouette outlined.
Silent hillside sentinel,
The sunset vista beautified.

Blossoms in springtime rains
Harbinger autumn claims
Of fruited harvests when
Leaves ablaze, bows bend low again.

The evergreen bower
White and emerald snow tower
Branches weighted to the ground,
The winter haven birds have found.

The warmth of human hearths,
Cooking heat for countless feasts,
Houses' sheltering source,
The body's final ark.

The Scarlet Tanager

There on the green grass
In brilliant light
He stood stock-still.
Jet black wings folded,
Scarlet body in radiant contrast,
Beyond belief, transfixing.
How long did boy and bird
Look at each other?
No way to tell,
So powerful the spell.
Only when he moved
Did the mind comprehend,
He was alive.
He took flight and disappeared.
In disbelief, the doubt,
Was it real?
Can such beauty exist?

From Pollywog to Frog

From the shallow water at the edge of the pond
The four-legged pollywog with the long tail
Stares at me as I stare back in wonderment
Of the transition taking place, a natural miracle.

Hummingbirds in Maine

We arrived at our lakeside camp the usual time, the last week of June.
The hummingbirds beat us there as usual, traveling a lot farther.
It took several days to hang the feeders in their usual place.
Before we had that chance, a hummingbird visited the empty space
Where the feeder usually hung, flying in a circle facing inward,
Toward the place where the feeder should have been.
Obviously he had been here before. Last summer, maybe even before.
After over a thousand-mile flight and a nine-month absence,
He found the exact spot, in an endless forest,
Where the previous feeder had hung from a small, birch tree branch.
Such a small brain, such a phenomenal feat.
An example of Creation's grandeur.

The Newborn

Transplanted from your sheltered home
    of darkened warmth and needs fulfilled,
Into a world of light and air,
    of love and hate, of hope, despair.

What do you think, see, feel, or hear?
    Are food and sleep your only needs?
What of the seeds planted deep within
    that are more than mere protein?

A million years of time in you combine
    to bridge the future with the past.
Head so large, fine fingers grasp mine;
    is there any doubt that you're divine?

The New Arrival

Only yesterday you were not here.
Preparation for earthly survival
Foretold your arrival.

From the unknown you came,
To which you will return
After life's short sojourn.

Your love lights this temporal space,
Some think it special,
Not knowing its source.

Loved because you're ours,
For what you may become,
Hope's redeemer, love's projection.

Love beyond special,
Corporeal reminder of
Love's universal splendor.

The First Day of School

I feel a little sad today,
A friend of mine has gone away.
They call it school,
But I'm no fool;
He's left his carefree, cloistered world
To stretch and grow in ways untold.
The ways that others think he should.

The Bike

When I was just a little tyke
I used to ride a three-wheeled bike
As I recall it was painted green,
Spokes and rims had a silver sheen.

When I grew up, when I was nine,
I got a bike for Christmas.
I still remember it as plain as
The Christmas morning then.

Painted red with big balloon tires,
Chrome handlebars, horn, light attired,
Kickstand and a rack on back
So books and papers could be stacked.

At first the bike a bit too large,
Twenty-six-inch wheels, steel frame took charge.
Careening out of a boy's control,
Safety in doubt, only balance extolled.

Skinned knees small price to pay,
Bleeding elbows given little heed
By fellows trying to
Master two-wheeled steeds.

I think it was at age fourteen
I had my bike dreams fulfilled.
Curved handlebars, racing tires,
Three gear, hill-flattening shifter.

Everywhere I now could go
With ease and skill and show,
The total blend of bike and boy,
No longer just a simple toy.

Fall

A kaleidoscope of colors paint the eye,
    leaf-strewn carpets of decaying red and gold.
Fragrant earth mists titillate the nose.
Smoldering smoke wisps drift from fields,
    lingering gray haze among the brilliant trees.
Autumnal sun's late, slanting rays
    lengthen shadows as daylight fades.
High in the sky, black dots fly,
    like schools of fish, the flocks wheel as one,
    southward, seeking food, soon no longer to be found.
In the stillness of early, falling night,
    full harvest moon glows orange-hued bright,
    silhouettes cornstalk stacks in ordered rows,
Brittle, dried sentinels, remnants of verdant life,
    honor guard to the approaching cold.

Winter Magic

Awakening at dawn, excitement stirs
As awareness of the stillness builds.
Night attired the day in quiet broad and deep.
Snow's insulation blankets ground, roof, iced pond,
Windowsill, muffled world in silence stilled.
Flakes fall slowly, steadily, from leaden sky,
Dampen, deflect, a distant crow's cry.
Soft virgin shroud of winter magic,
Transformer of adult-world tasks
Restorer of beauty to a withered land.

Cycles

Raindrops form into rivulets,
Combine to make high mountain streams,
Crystal clear, fast-moving murmur,
Infant start of the long journey,
Coursing through countless turns,
Roaring over waterfalls and cataracts,
Gliding beneath golden bows, around smooth stones,
In whirlpool swirls and quiet pools,
Between widened banks slow and deep,
Only to disappear, enfolded in the sea.
As moisture rises into wind-formed clouds,
A new cycle begins again.
The raindrop never lost.

On Watson Pond

Each day the lake, a changing scene,
Kaleidoscopic timeless interplay of light.
Glacial rocks at rest ten thousand years,
Half buried, ice scarred
Stoic reminders of a distant past,
Shadowed now by light, new forests cast.
Wind ripples race across the lake,
Invite bowed bank birches
To a rustling playful dance.
A chipmunk's hurried hungered pace,
Undaunted in its purposeful race.
The hummingbird's distinctive whir
Proclaims a sunbathed red-green blur
From leafy bower to wildflower,
Long-beaked nectar feeder,
Incidental plant breeder.
A sapsucker's cat-like call
Interrupts its tattooed taps.
Close by, the phoebe calls its name.
A loon asserts its territorial rights,
Sending mother merganser into startled flight.
Yellow and white water lilies open and close
On cycled tides of light, as day displaces night.
Mirror calm glazes the lake as day awakes.
Still-winged turkey vultures mount thermal risers,
As cloud shadows glide on wooded hills.
A frog's hoarse croak echoes in the quiet night.
Star flicker sprinkles the sky's dark arch.
The Milky Way the center span,
Blended countless points of light,

Whose outer edge is home.
Camouflaged against the brown-gray rock
A water snake basks in its solar bath.
Legs outstretched, a turtle floats,
Snout just out, mistaken for a log.
Deeper still, schools of sleek fishes mill.
Rain first heard in woods across the lake
Advances at a quickened pace,
Ruffled water, near shore vaulted,
Metal camp roof assaulted.
Dripping leaves disguise the end,
As dark clouds still scurry by,
'Til sunlight refracted from each rainbowed drop
Ends the turbulent interlude,
Refreshed fragrant quietude.

The Rocks on Pemaquid Point

On slanted edge upended stand
The rocks on Pemaquid Point,
Was it glaciers fifty thousand years ago
Or some subterranean thrust
That created this coastline thus?
Granite structures frozen in time,
Standing firm against the pounding surf
In mortal battle, these stalwart foes
Test their strength to reveal nature's will.
Sand beaches elsewhere foretell
The gradual change time's outcome spells.
In time all things change.
No permanence here to find
Despite the sensory deception.

The Wind

Unseen force, known only by its effects,
Moaning at the tree's resistance,
Scattering leaves into piles and snow into drifts,
Driving waves against the seawall, incessant thundering,
Slanting the rain, turning umbrellas inside out,
Driving ships aground, destroying homes, overturning cars,
Bending, twisting trees around before they hit the ground,
Planes and birds grounded by its mighty gusts,
Sometimes so still it is unseen, felt, or heard,
Only to arise again, a restless, unending force.
Blessed cooling whisper on hot sultry nights,
Unwelcome cold draft on frigid wintry days.
Howling down chimney flues,
Whistling in the rigging of tall sailing ships
Now becalmed, then driven madly into the mounting waves.
Carrier of fragrant blossom smells, vehicle of acid rain.
Whisperer of the season's change.

Winter's End

Snow was falling gently while the sun journeyed north again,
A great, white, silent, blanket bedded winter in.
In the white pine grove, a red flash of color glows,
The crest-headed cardinal flits among the trees.

Crocus sleep deep beneath the snow, their chromatic splendor
Wait freedom from winter's frigid fist held tight,
Awakened from the long night by spring's warmth and light,
As sun and earth conspire to bring forth nature's new attire

Transcendence

Pines stretch tall against a leaden sky
As though holding the earth's ceiling high.
Against emerald boughs snowflakes contrast,
Each branch, in crystal splendor cast.

The sun from behind breaks through,
Each tree glistening in light anew.
A red cardinal flashes within the bower,
In contrast to the green-white towers.

Isolated from this world somehow,
Apart from this natural home,
Separated by self-absorption,
Detached from full participation.

Then that special moment comes,
The ego melts, replaced by
The new Self, emerging.
Creation's call, excluding nothing at all.

Spring

The silent snows have come and gone,
Rivulets swell the streams,
Cresting the mighty rivers' banks.

The sun climbs slowly higher every day,
March gusts voice the season's change.
Does time stand still, or have buds swelled again?

The patient grow inpatient, the impetuous despair.
Then, a hint of green: it's here,
Beneath the lawn's dead brown.

Spring Scene

Forsythia and daffodils early
in spring's unfolding scene,
Yellow splashes against
lawn's verdant green.
Soon magnolia and tulip too
add color to the changing view.
Then dogwood and azalea come along;
robins add their joyous song.
Later, the multicolored rose
announce spring's close.
The whole performance
lasts a month or so,
Like the circus,
it annually comes and goes.

The Cathedral

The sun shines in multicolored patterns
On the ancient, pilgrim-worn, stone floor.
The whole interior infused with soft-colored light,
The perfect vision of Heaven's waiting delight.
Soaring arches appear to carry one to dizzying heights,
Stone and wood carvings made with meticulous care
Attract the eye at every turn, reinforcing
Themes in wall paintings and glowing stained glass.
Constructed over hundreds of years,
Generations worked but never saw it done.
Admired now and for generations still to come.
Spirit encased in glass, stone, design, and art,
Cultural monument to the power of God.

The skyscraper is our culture's counterpart,
Monument to a belief in materialism,
Functionalism without spiritual art.
A stained environment instead of stained glass.
Where is the Divine in the scientific mind?

Florence

Florence in the summer
Full of all those others
There to see all the same things
And go to all the same places,
But oh what things and places!
Could any man create those statues?
Others have but not like these.
The great dome, the bridges,
The city spilling over the river.
An escape from the present,
A translation in time,
A cultural shift,
All preserved in a city
That hallows its past.
Smaller than Rome,
Bigger than Assisi,
Its grandeur expands
With each walk in its streets,
And each person you meet.
Like the Muslims to Mecca
The heirs of the Renaissance
Make their pilgrimage
To Florence to renew their faith.

Venice

From island refuge to city-state
That took a thousand years.
Then another four hundred
To the sometimes-flooded city
Of tourist delight,
Where the Po and Piave Rivers
Meet the Adriatic Sea.
From Saint Mark Square
To the Rialto Bridge,
Wind the intricate canals,
Lined with palaces,
Like the Ca'D'Oro.
Magnificent architecture,
Byzantine, Gothic, Renaissance,
Contain the voluptuous women of Titian,
The religious art of Tintoretto.
Romance, history, beauty,
Replete in this unique City
Built on piles driven into
The mud of a hundred islands.
Traversed by gondolas that stop
At doors open to the water,
Pass under uncounted bridges
In their unhurried journeys.
Gone are the great warships,
The merchant fleets,
Along with the great Princes.
Yet the time capsule
Of their affluence remains
To entertain years later,
Lord Byron, Robert Browning,
You and me.

Beauty

Grand vistas witness beauty's verdant bloom,
Overwhelmed by pulse-quickening delight consumed.
While calm pools of contemplation provide
Inner tranquility, where quiet beauty resides.
Stillness that leads to knowing within
Reveals the source of which outer beauty is akin.
Unity of the outer and inner worlds
Confirms the divinity all things herald.

Bridging the Gap

Each encapsulated in steel and glass,
Enmeshed in the frustration of a traffic jam,
Separated by their shared animosity.
Each minute of immobility accumulates,
As unfocused anger looks for a victim.
A horn blows, one lane moves, the other stalls.
Then, in a car slowly rolling past,
A child smiles and waves.
The anger that separation permits
Vanishes as the gap is closed
By the inclusiveness that love permits.

What Use?

The blue of the sky
Seen in mind's eye,
The smell of a rose,
The touch of the wind
Felt on the skin,
Of what use are these?

A fond embrace
That makes the heart race,
The night sky's wonderment,
The surf's tireless roar
That makes spirit soar,
Of what use are these?

A quiet moment in the woods
Where native Indians stood,
The laughing brook disturbs.
The Loon's wild calls
Recall northern summer lakes,
Of what use are these?

With a grander eye
That sees beyond the sky
Into the heart of All,
The soul records beyond mind's recall
The true meaning often missed
Oh what use are these!

Why?

Oh why do I keep asking why?
Why am I? Why life? Why death?
Why this universe of billions of stars
That stretch beyond imagining?
Why this sun, this earth, this moon?

Science tells how but never why,
Sometimes how not so well either.
Newspapers are good at when, where, who,
But seem never concerned with why.
So why is it so important to you and me?

To some, the answer to why is simply God.
"Why God?" ask I, in uneasy uncertainty.
Is it just arrogance to always be asking why?
Is it true what sages say:
"We can never really know anything"?

Is it enough to merely accept that I am?
Is it meant for man not to understand?
If all my energy goes into being,
Living, loving, creating, helping,
There's no reason for why; it's enough to be.

So to know is not answered by asking why.
To know is gained through the experience of being.
To feel the reality of what we are,
Not an intellectual answer to endless whys
But a knowledge gained through living what we are.

Why is such a seductive trap I fall into it every day?
Why can't I realize it is just a dead end?
Oh I've just done it again!
Is there nothing that will save me
From this intellectual game I play?

Born 1896

Born in a house with kerosene lamps,
An outhouse in the backyard,
A wood stove for cooking and heat,
A hand pump for water and a horse in the barn.
Newspapers the sole source of news.
Books the source of knowledge.
Doctors made house calls
Yet three of the family died of TB.
Railroads revolutionized transportation on land,
While steamboats replaced sails at sea.
Immigrants, including his parents, streamed into the country.

Before he died in 1979, he witnessed tremendous
Technological changes unprecedented in a lifetime.
The telephone, the automobile, the airplane, the lightbulb,
The moving picture, the radio, television, central heating,
Indoor plumbing, X-ray machines, refrigerators,
Freezers, toasters, stoves, mixers, and countless others.
The atomic bomb was exploded and electricity generated by the atom.
Antibiotics revolutionized medicine,
Men walked on the moon and saw the earth from outer space.
Cities were urbanized and farmers industrialized.
The Union expanded to include six new states.
The birth of the computer, the dawn of the communication age.

Still, through it all, a father, husband, breadwinner,
A W.W. I survivor of the technological horror of trench warfare,
At Bell Labs a helper to develop sonar in W.W. II,
A lover of life and family, changed by it all, yet unchanged still.
What does it take to change the soul of man? Or does it change?

Hello Dolly

One age is ending, another begins.
Mankind is over, womankind has begun.
The stem cell has replaced the sperm.
The reality of the clone is known.
In sheep, then monkeys,
Can humans be far behind?
The president says it's unethical.
Christians say it's immoral.
Muslims feel it's okay.
What are we to say?

Does a clone have a soul?
Is it the same or different?
Or is a body a body
And a soul a soul.
Is a clone just an identical twin?
So what's the big deal?
We have plenty of them.
Simply put, humans have never
Reproduced asexually before.
Is it the end for man and evolution,
Or just a new twist in the way we exist?

An Ode to Brandy

Steadfast friend throughout life.
Love unwavering to the end.
Beauteous presence gone forever,
Void filled only with memory's essence.

Trust-filled life of devotion.
Never a complaint, not even a sigh.
Brown eyes, soul shinning through,
Offering unqualified love for you.

The bond between man and dog
Is special, caring, very strong.
Strengthened in each act of giving,
Enriching both in mutual loving.

The Cat and the Chipmunk

The chipmunk passed my door each day,
Going someplace from somewhere else.
Places known only to him but not to me.
In passing, he stopped to gather seeds
Against winter's scarcity soon to come.
Then one day, a tiger cat appeared,
In a mad rush, his presence made known.
Now the chipmunk comes no more.
Absent caller at my lakefront door.
Seeds so laboriously put away
Unneeded in his abbreviated stay.

On Visiting a Florida Wildlife Preserve

The world we knew as a child has gone away,
Replaced by unpleasant realities taught today.
Ceaseless change seems its eternal way.
Fear and uncertainty in the mind holds sway.

Survival of the fittest has won,
Nature demonstrates it with everyone.
The food chain leaving out not a single one.
No guiltless basking in the sun.

Death seems to be the way of life.
Existence just one endless strife.
Extinction, life's unwanted wife.
Evolution's story everywhere in sight.

But what of this friendlier world we knew,
Before science destroyed our naive view?
Secure and loving, optimism renewed,
Real? Imagined? Or simplicity gone askew?

Belief is all that's in the mind.
It selects what's out there to find.
Choose carefully what is deified,
Or faith in life will be undermined.

Survival of the fittest, aggression's recipe.
Altruism, the survivor in love's legacy.
Maybe we should look again to find
What at first escaped our inner mind.

The Revolution

The statue topples from its base,
Decapitated upon impact with the street,
Symbolic end to tyranny's grip.
But the pieces, oh the pieces!
Can Humpty Dumpty be put together again?

Every end is a new beginning.
What needs to be ended is often clear,
Sometimes the new is harder to define.
Still harder, the recognition that
Change brings loss as well as gain.

Into the vacuum of indecision
Comes immediate opportunism,
Blind to future ideals,
Callous to the well-being of others,
Focused only on the greed of now.

While the founding fathers
Struggle to create the new,
Will the masses put up with the now,
Or will the short-term greed
Annihilate long-term liberty?

Slavery, Bondage, Exploitation

Slavery no longer legal in America,
But bondage and exploitation flourish.
Its resource illegal immigration,
Its perpetrators unethical employers,
Its victims migrant farmworkers,
Women in the sex industry,
And all undocumented immigrants.
Where is the freedom in economic slavery?

The economics of education and housing
And its resultant segregation
Bind the poor to inadequate opportunity,
Perpetuates bondage and exploitation
From generation to generation.
Color, race, ethnicity, religion,
Fellow travelers, not the cause.
Where is the freedom in lack of opportunity?

Political power held by the wealthy
Keep borders porous to illegals,
Providing low-cost manpower,
Often with boarder-crossing debts,
Indenturing them for years
To low-paying jobs.
The new "company town" now national.
Where is the freedom in political disenfranchisement?

The Two-Sided Coin

Rights and responsibilities
Are a two-sided coin.
The exercise of every right has consequences.
The right to swing your arms on a picket line
Ends where the other person's nose begins.
Do no harm is simultaneously
The right and responsibility of all.
Responsibility is granting to all others
The same rights we claim for ourselves.
Deny others their rights,
And soon it will become your rights denied.
"To give is more blessed than to receive."
For rights: "To give IS to receive."
Responsibility is behaving so as
Not to violate any right we cherish.

TV Culture

The culture depicted on TV
Constricts our mind to only find
Sex and violence of every kind.

The distorted world TV presents
Is one that every one resents,
Yet passively each of us consents.

The paranoia it can create
Fosters fear, distrust, and hate,
Making life an unhappy state.

Get up; turn off the set.
There's time to love life yet!
Live before you're laid to rest.

Time 1

Time, always a fickle dimension,
Seems quicker in its rate of late.
I try hard to understand it,
But it's beyond me to comprehend its pace.

When I retired, the need for an alarm clock expired,
Along with life's hectic rat race.
I knew I would find time for the list in my mind,
Those countless undone tasks from the past.

But the list seems to grow exponentially,
While time seems to shrink, despite what I think.
Then others ask, "What do you do? Are you bored?"
What can I say? Tell them time has faded away?

Maybe it's just that as life proceeds,
Everything else becomes older, too.
Each requiring repair, demanding more care,
But that can't account for time running out.

Then I thought, time hasn't changed,
It's what remains that's not the same.
So much behind, so little ahead,
The imbalance makes the present more urgent.

Perhaps as death draws nearer,
Time quickens its pace in this unavoidable race,
Pushed by fear of the end and the shortening course,
The time that remains seems too short to avert the loss.

It's ironic somehow that the more alive,
Faster time seems to fly, yet death arrives no sooner.
Life is never long enough when it's you who dies.
With life and death, no compromise; oh how time flies!

Time 2

The illusion of the ego
As a separate entity
Demands the existence
Of serial time
To maintain the delusion.

We seem to exist
In three time frames,
Yesterday, today, and tomorrow.
A fantasy of the ego,
For now is all there is.

Eternity is the only reality,
An unbroken time dimension
Of past, present, and future,
Extending infinitely
In the spiritual domain.

In it, all are united with all.
There can be no separation
Without time's existence.
Distance requires time.
Separation requires distance.

There is only one time
And it is now.
There is no yesterday,
No tomorrow,
Now is the only time there is.

2006 CE

We call this year 2006 CE, for the Christian era.
Why not 2484 CE, for the Confucian era?
Or 1436 ME, for the Mohammedan era.
Or maybe 2569 BE, for the Buddhist era.
Don't be fooled by the labels.
The ever-present now is all there is.
There is no past or future, only the infinite now.
Be here now. As though we had a choice.
So Happy Now Year.
Or should I merely say, Happy Now?
Since the year is an arbitrary period of time
Taken by this infinitesimal speck of dust we call Earth
To travel around a third-rate star we call the sun,
One of hundreds of billions of stars in the Universe.
Oh well, Happy New Year anyway.

What Time Is It?

What time is it to be?
Time to be completely free
To answer the call of destiny.

Time to come home
To the One we've known
Before the ego was enthroned.

Time to share love's gift,
Heal mankind's rift,
Reverse our separatist drift.

Time to stand with all others,
Treat each as equal brothers,
As to all the earth is mother.

Time to stop exploitation,
Enhance world cooperation,
Revive earth's habitation.

Time to know we are interdependent.
Not one a separate segment,
Bound together in love resplendent.

Time to know that in the end,
Only love will replace and mend
The hostility men often seem to intend.

Time to know one's born to heal
The separation we all feel,

As our true Spirit is revealed.

Live in the Universal Light.
Share its limitless might,
To pierce the isolation of our night.

Music

For me, it's Mozart.
The simple, complex beauty,
The lightness, the humor,
The expected yet magically unexpected,
The enthusiastic productivity,
The endless stream of creativity,
The shared delight,
The nonverbal awareness
Of our selfless selves,
The bridge of time
Captured in this
Unity of presence.
Thank you, Mozart
For opening windows of the Soul.

Music and the Soul

Music and the soul interact.
Energy is the common source.
Vibrations at complex frequencies
Inherent in musical scores
Dampen, enhance, vibration
Frequencies of the soul.
Every chakra vibrates at its own rate,
Each musical instrument at its own frequency,
These interactions stimulate aspects of our being,
Affecting our perceptions and emotions.
Traditionally, specific instruments
Are associated with different chakras.
So in complex ways, rhythms, melodies, instrumentation,
Interact with chakra frequencies,
Arousing the base of spiritual responses.
Musical energy and cosmic energy
All parts of the seamless whole of Creation.

Survival's Creed

A temporary custodial thread
In nature's timeless web,
Let me not be the destructive threat
That weakens the interdependent net.

Nothing each does need raise fears,
So little a contribution, it appears,
Yet, countless species disappear,
Thoughtless acts build their bier.

Each individual act so small,
Hundred-year-old trees in minutes fall.
In the hands of men, so many saws!
Oxygen still needed for the breath of all.

Every act affects me and all others, too.
I'm responsible for everything I do
To this generation and each anew.
Can mutual dependence become our view?

The Choice Is Ours

We choose how we see ourselves.
A finite speck blowing in the universe,
Or a spiritual partner of the Divine.
If thinking is confined to the sensory world,
We know ourselves as a material body.
If open to other perceptions,
We believe we are something more.

As we sense our body's energy field,
We know materialism is insufficient.
How can it explain acupuncture and the placebo affect,
Faith and psychic healing,
How warts are cured or hypnotic blisters caused,
How people walk on glowing coals,
Neither feeling pain nor being injured.

To create a new understanding
Perception needs to expand
To realize the spiritual dimension.
We are what we perceive ourselves to be.
To expand our concept of self,
We must open to new awareness.
The choice: to be blind or see.

Waking Up

Leisure Time

White beaches stretch mile on mile,
Bordering the surf's inviting smile.
Stay and tarry for a while.
Waves murmur in a soothing hum,
Bask in the warm topical sun,
Imagine nothing but leisure fun.
Stretch in the sand, be a bum.
Eyelids flicker, the breath steadies,
Gentle breezes caress the skin,
Distractions now seem petty.
The surf murmurs, don't care, don't care,
Drift off to a state less aware,
Where time and place disappear
Within the sun-bright glare
Of closed eyelid's stare.

The Family

Totally dependent in dark, warm sheltering.
Then for years, the family was the total world.
Soon, the culture expanded awareness
To neighbor, city, nation, and beyond.
The astronomers reached beyond the earth
To solar system, galaxy, universe.
The philosophers and mystics explored the inner space
Of values, ethics, belief, spirituality, and enlightenment.
Where does the family of man's dependency end?
Perhaps there is no beginning or end,
Just expanded awe and humility
At Creation's scope, magnificence, and interdependence.

The Generations

Children, the future's perfect gift
To all whom time leaves behind.
Each generation's loss replaced
With restless youth's unquenchable zest.

Each generation's passing
Seems a fresh renewal instead,
Forever a new wave's crest,
In humanity's endless quest.

What beach is this, the waves assault,
Soft sands of comfort and leisure,
Rocky shores of conflict and strife,
Quiet harbor of wisdom and insight?

Crosscurrents run deep in life's sea,
Prevent not the high tide's flow.
As life's high-water peaks,
Each thinks he's found that which he seeks.

Still the fruitless search goes on,
Where only chaos seems to be,
The world's high tide but deceives,
Too soon again it does recede.

No two alike, yet all the same,
In birth and death and in between,
Knowing not from where we come
Nor how or when we will succumb.

Yet we think we're in control.
If only we could clearly know
The meaning of this world we see,
At peace would generations be.

The Courage to Be

Each individual a separate spark of consciousness,
Yet part of the total light of humanity.
In sharing each individual awareness,
The collective experience of humanity
Expands, benefiting all by adding to the light.
It takes courage to be open and honest,
But this is the only way humanity
Moves toward its ultimate destiny
Of universal enlightenment.
Have the courage to be!

The Law of Opposites

The senses only know of material things,
But mind is not so confined.
As long as mind stays sensory bound,
Only the Law of Opposites will be found.
To free itself of sensory limits
The mind must turn deep within,
Only then will the unity be attained
That transcends the world of appearances.
As awareness of the Spiritual Self evolves
The world of opposites dissolves.

The Wheel of Life

Life's outer rim is a ceaseless doing,
As it attempts to satisfy desires,
Instead, creating only new ones,
Creating endless cycles of doing and desiring.

Its center is a motionless void,
Into which God fits,
Supplying all knowing.
Where are you,
At the center or the rim?

In Defense of the Irrational

Rational ego mind creates a myriad of choices,
Assuring the importance of its continued existence.
Choosing, desiring, doing; its endless cycle of change.
Fear arises in this ceaseless merry-go-round.
Ego identifies with the body and fears its demise.
Yet, death of the body is an inevitable end.

There is only one choice: between fear and love.
Love is the state of our being eternally unchanging,
Irrational beyond reasoned understanding,
A state of peace and bliss beyond words,
Known by transcending the rational mind.
Stay only in the rational, and fear is your companion.

Surrender to Salvation

What do we really know?
At first, it seems so much.
Science has a long list
That demonstrates its powers.

The ego invests in them.
Knowledge seems abundant,
Until we ask questions
For which no one has answers.

What is the meaning of existence?
Who am I? Is there a God?
What happens when I die?
Am I only a physical being?

We realize to answer these,
Scientific knowledge is folly.
Because the sensory world
Is only partial knowledge.

Transcendent truth goes beyond
The sensory world of things.
Truth is gained within the mind
Through silent remembering.

Truth

What is truth?
Is it any more
Than temporal belief
Transitory, ever changing,
Always thought to be
If not ultimate
At least more correct?

An anthropomorphic God
Replaced by scientific materialism
Whose definition of material
Now thought to constitute
Only a small percentage
Of the total cosmos,
Such a little "truth"!

A belief in scarcity
And individual competition,
One person's gain
Another person's loss,
Exploitation of nature
To satisfy greed,
Nature's balance distorted.

There is another
Way to believe,
Permanent, everlasting,
Unaltered by the new ideas
Of scientific discovery,
Based not on material existence
But on transcendent values.

Love is the ground
Of our existence.
That done for one
Is done for all.
There is no scarcity.
Love, creativity, forgiveness
Are limitless, without end.

Is Belief All There Is?

Is knowledge anything other than belief?
Can anything be proven beyond belief?
Is science more than consensual belief?
Is faith more than belief in the unprovable?
Beliefs are our codified perceptions of the world,
And the world we know is created by them.
Beliefs are shared and thus become the beliefs of others.
Beliefs are the structural pillars of consciousness.
What is the nature of conscious awareness beyond belief?

Diversity and Separateness

The more diverse a culture the greater
Are the perceived differences between individuals.
These differences foster separation and encourage projection.
Projection transfers responsibility and blame to others.

Introspection and the realization of the true Self are blocked.
Knowing the true Self dispels the illusion of separateness.
This realization of the oneness of humanity in diversity
Is the Divine Self, shared by all.

One Light

The world of appearances
Is an array of bewildering differences,
Each difference a pair of opposites.
Judgments of good and bad
Constantly confront us
As we choose between them
Based on our cultural biases.

So caught are we in these judgments
We lose sight of the light
Shining behind these shadows.
This light knows no differences.
Beyond the shadows
Of our self-imposed limits
This Eternal Light radiates
The perfect Unity that is our true Being.

The Risk Worth Taking

To remove the padlock from perception's door
Opens dangerous territory to explore.
Although the door opens only a crack,
Forever there is no turning back.

The analysts say there is much to fear
With repressed emotions everywhere.
The shadows of the rejected self
Fearfully clutter personal history's shelf.

The yogis offer a transcendent view
Of what each has to do.
Concentrate and quiet the mind,
Seek inner peace; leave turmoil behind.

When Kundalini is properly aroused,
In the crown chakra it becomes housed,
Enlightenment and liberation the guarantee,
Now and for eternity.

From ego self to Self-realization,
Path of universal participation,
Some slowly, some fast, but each at last
Untie the ego knot of personal past.

Firstborn

Your stillborn cry choked
By the cord around your throat,
Soundless, deep-felt loss,
Lifeless, life-altering force,
Lost love's lingering pain,
Unseen, unknown, unforgotten.
Firstborn hopes, dreams, demands
All lost, gone, every careful plan
Undone before it began.

Looking back across time's span
The pain recedes, hidden away,
The terrible loss now seen as gain.
The messenger brought another map
To plot a different course,
Long journey
Away from personal power,
To find instead the unseen thread
Connecting love to every event.

Death Watch

Each labored breath's struggle for life
Pierces deep the troubled hearts that watch.
So painful the stay,
The family turns away.

Then a sudden dramatic switch
From the fight for life,
A quiet peace ascends
From a place where serenity transcends.

So profound this change of state,
Death's mystery grips all in awe.
Life no longer asserts demands,
Tranquil death quietly takes command.

A Mother's Death

There is no separation more desperately felt
Than the death of our mother.
No human relationship has been more intimate,
More dependent, more loving, more nurturing.
Yet who of us, after the opportunity is past,
Feel we expressed our gratitude adequately.
Perhaps it is the irreversible finality of death
That makes this separation so difficult.
Think of the many other separations in life.
First, the separation from the mother's body,
Then from the breast and later from the home.
Each of these had its own pain.
Yet each offered, for both mother and child,
Opportunities for growth and development.
Does death, the ultimate separation, offer anything less?
Most of us have difficulty in seeing these opportunities,
Clouded as they are by the pain of loss.
Only after time will their spiritual reality emerge,
To be fulfilled in some way now unanticipated.
Within the mind and soul there is a bridge.
In love there is no real separation.

Only the Body

It's the body that dies, you say.
"ONLY the body?" I ask.
This thing I've been feeding all these years,
Exercising, tanning, admiring, displaying,
With clothing to enhance its appeal?
The same body the doctor checks?
The one people identify as me?
ONLY this dies, you say,
What else can there be?

It's wrong to think of the body as me,
I'm so much more, you say.
But without a body, can I be me?
The body is the house I live in,
I'm the resident, not the house, you say.
But all my effort is in house maintenance,
"Who cares for the resident?" I ask.
What care is needed except to know
Who the homeowner really is?

The Body

Transcend your body.
Know belief in it is a sham.
If you invest in it,
You will never understand.

The world of things
Includes it, too,
And when it's gone,
What's left, if that is you?

Know yourself as something more
Than the body's material shell.
Seek deep within yourself
For the light that knows you well.

That light dispels all darkness,
Peace your natural inner feeling.
That light shines in all of us,
Our transcendent spiritual being.

The Ultimate Choice

Is there something else to do,
Love to share, despair to bear,
A helping hand, or a tender reprimand?
Is there something to learn, a fear to spurn,
A sunset to see, in the stillness to be,
A confession to make, high ground to take?
Let the energy flow, so the body will know
If it's still needed here to sustain life another year.

The decision is only yours to make.
Fear not; death has nothing to take.
Listen to what your spirit knows,
Its wisdom with creation flows.

If soul decides it wants to stay,
The body can have it no other way.
If instead you decide it's time to go,
In love, not fear, let it be so.

A Change in Plan

The suet feeder's call too strong to resist,
The downy pecked away, calories against a cold day.

He went to work at McDonald's,
Same as every day, money for food and rent.

The hawk swooped down and picked him off,
So fast, the blur was hard to see.

The bandit came, they say, at twelve,
Laid them on the floor, head to head.

The talons clutched and squeezed,
Wings fluttered slowly, then were still.

The gunman straddled them
And fired two shots.

The hawk flew off, meal in tow,
Suet feeder hanging still.

Two men not returning home,
Groceries still to buy.

Death

Oh death, to all your visit comes,
To some too soon, to others late,
But from your grasp, none escape.
The strong, the brave, the weak, the ill
Are all the same, your quota filled.
There is no ransom to be paid,
Good works, brave deeds, all paid no heed.
So what is there of meaning left,
When your visit makes us all bereft?
Who testifies against you, when
After you come, you've silenced them?
From the stillness, is there a call?
Spirit's voice, freed from the shroud,
To pierce your veil of doom,
To reveal a changeless, immortal Self,
Abiding ever, concealed within,
Unknown to our restricted view.
Transcendent Self resplendent,
Spiritual Light brightly glowing,
Survivor of the body's demise,
Radiant ray of eternal sunrise.

The Graveyard

Headstones for centuries stand guard
Against time's erosion of the past.
Granite markers of fragile memories'
Futile attempt to last.

The date of birth, the date of death,
The years stretching in between,
No mystery now, their length clearly seen.
Some short, some long, what can it mean?

Relentlessly time fades the dates,
As years recede, the letters blur,
Hiding who occupied each niche
In time's endless tide.

So little left behind to remind
Us of each life's contribution.
Perhaps the graveyard's not the place to look.
But where? Some might suggest in history books.

The "great" deeds of some recorded there,
But what of all the others lying here?
Row on row with names and dates,
The little deeds of many uncounted with the "great."

What meaning then to life
If this is all that remains?
Testimony to individual mortality,
All ending here the same.

Are the flowers and the flags
A clue to some lasting effect?
Or are they just more transitory
Than the gravestones' fading names and dates?

The Holocaust Museum

It wasn't easy to force oneself to go,
you knew how hard it would be
to expose the dark side we all deny.
Humanity capable of such depravity,
almost beyond comprehension.
Yet, there it is for all to see.
Anger at being part of the same race,
frustration that so little was done,
amazement at the fearlessness of the too few,
the realization that it can happen again,
the mindless obedience to authority,
the unquestioning loyalty to the state,
man's infinite capacity for evil,
the hell man's unfathomed cruelty can create.

Buried within the ashes of this blackest hour,
though almost out yet still flickering low,
Love's light can faintly be discerned
in the compassionate acts of the loving few.
What motivates such courage and self-sacrifice?
Is it their recognition that all are One?
Is it the realization that death holds no sting?
Or knowing that one is already the walking dead
with nothing left to lose
but still having something left to give?
Does this stripping away reveal the true Self?
Can this be seen as love triumphant?
Let us pray we all can find the way.

Afraid to Die?

Afraid to die? Well, so was I
Until I thought about it.

A child is born, nobody mourns.
Somehow, a birth seems different.

Death's threshold crossed, a friend is lost,
Or so it seems to be.

If everyone born in the early morn
Sails forth at dusk on death's calm sea,

How then can birth and death be seen so differently?
Each just end points of personal history.

From the unknown we all have come,
Only to return at the end again.

Life without death is like life without breath.
Accept life and death is a certainty.

What is there to fear? Is this life so dear
That new ventures cannot be dared?

Choose Life

Overcoming the fear of death
Is not affirmed by suicide.
Suicide places death on a pedestal,
Elevating its significance over life.
True loss of the fear of death
Creates the freedom to embrace life totally.
Creates the realization there is only life
And death is only of the physical body,
Opening the way for complete fulfillment in life.
Physical death is unavoidable
And comes soon enough for all.
But it cannot be shared,
Because it is the symbol of loss.
Life is the gift to be shared.
Use the physical body to communicate
The love we create in life.

The Fear of Loss

All fear is the fear of loss.
Fear's list of loss is endless:
Loss of special relationships:
Spouse, children, father, mother,
Loss of job, money, prestige, prosperity,
Loss of direction, destiny, meaning,
Loss of self-esteem, self-worth, value,
Loss of health, happiness, joy.
Fear generated by our false attachment
To the apparent reality of life's impermanence.
The greater one's possessions,
The higher the level of achievement,
The stronger the tie to others,
The more one has to lose.
All the treasures of this life pass away,
Stolen by the death of the body.
The soul's treasures have permanence,
Remaining always in the Universal Mind.
Every loving thought there preserved
In the light of their own perfect radiance.
All the past except its beauty gone,
All your kindnesses remain,
Beyond destruction and guilt.
The Peace of God is in your heart,
To hold and share always.
Learn to love the permanent.
Learn to let the impermanent go.

Glorious Greed

Oh gorious greed,
Fuel of economic life,
Product of scarcity's fear,
Goad to competition,
Cause of inequity.

Greed, scarcity, fear,
Trilogy confirmed
In poverty's plight,
Security sough in wealth,
Prestige and power's might.

The world the source,
Material goods the means,
But when wealth's center
Is found devoid,
Revealed a spiritual void.

A hole, no worldly goods can fill,
Though coffers flow with gold.
Nourished in another way,
Unmeasured by material gain,
Mended instead by invisible threads.

Woven in brotherhood,
Secured with love's knot,
Path of ultimate worth,
Base of unspoken wisdom,
Bond of universal trust.

The meaning of existence
Lies beyond material greed,
In deeply planted spiritual seeds,
Nurtured by compassionate deeds,
Flowering only in love's exchange.

The Hard Lesson

Death as an event rather than an end
Is a perception of freedom from fear.
To take off a pair of tight-fitting shoes,
Or like the snake shed an outgrown skin
Is only an end for what's left behind.
To awake in the morning leaves darkness for light,
The world of dreams for sense perception.
The body at birth imposes self-limitation
Transcended only with difficulty in life.
Death removes the limitation once again.
If we think of ourselves as the skin of the snake,
Or perhaps the pair of tight-fitting shoes,
We are trapped in a misperception of identity,
And death becomes the end so many fear.
Experience with death is a most powerful teacher
Of who we are and is not to be avoided,
Even though it seems so painful
When confronted in the deaths of others.
By repression and avoidance we inadvertently
Perpetuate the ignorance and fear of our false identity.
Death as an event, a transition of self-hood
Is no more to be feared than all those other
Developmental stages of life-offering opportunities
For self-enlargement and enhancement.
Let death teach us who we are.

Transition

Together we approach the Great Divide.
One soon to step across to the other side,
The other, here to temporarily reside.
Each helping the other as teacher and learner,
We confront the mystery all must face.
With an open mind, fear moves aside,
Making room for shared love to abide.
Exploring life between birth and death,
Seeing each as transition, not beginning and end.
Birth, the end of one unknown mystery,
Death, the beginning of mystery anew.
Each a great transition of consciousness
Within which life's constant change extends.
Despite the pain, discomfort, medication,
There is learning, teaching, loving, developing,
Joy unconquered, the spiritual quest unquenched.
At last, embraced by the love that knows no end,
The great transformation is fulfilled.

The Ripples of Creation

In endless rows, waves approach the coast,
Cresting, scattering spray and foam, crashing against the shore,
A defining roar; then in silence, they are no more,
Absorbed again into the sea from whence they came,
The endless sea, the separate waves all one.
One is born, treads the path of life from birth to death,
A separate wave in the ripple of Creation.

The Healing

From the blue light comes a green ray,
Touching the chest where the melanoma lay.
A wordless knowing communicates
You need not die to be with God.

No matter what happens, it's all right.
You live, you die, no reason for fright.
The spirit that is You, God will never smite.
Eternally in love, Self with God unite.

What is there to fear? God is as near
As the moment of knowing; He's not aloof.
Separated no longer from the love you crave.
Love, by death, can never be shattered.

The Most Powerful Illusion

It is God's Will
That you are well.
If in your present state
That seems not the case,
It means your will
And God's are separate.

This illness just
A shift in wills
From God's to yours.
The cure, a shift
From yours to His
Safe, Loving Embrace.

Since your will,
Separate from His,
Does not really exist,
Your illness is
Unreal as well
Despite what senses tell.

The hardest test
Of trust we face is
Created by the illness
Separation makes,
A powerful force
To heal our faith.

The cure, God's Loving Embrace:
I am created by God's Love.

I am sustained by God's Love.
I am protected by God's Love.
I am surrounded by God's Love.
I am ever becoming God's Love.

The Transcendental

Beyond the limits of our own time,
The blind spots of our cultural rhyme,
We only have to look within to find
Peace and love always in our mind,
Because God resides in all humankind.

In Pursuit of a Phantom

All truth passes through the filter of individual consciousness,
A consciousness formed by experience,
Forged in the cauldron of culture and family,
Prey to diverse internal and external forces,
Creating reality by perception and projection.
This is the truth we know, confirmed
By sharing it with others of the same belief.
How fragile this truth is
Based on place, time, and circumstance.
Yet, how certain we feel about what we think we know,
Deception concealed within the mind of the knower,
Only to be uncovered as new truth is discovered.
The new, all too soon, will also succumb to change.
Reality seems to rest on the shifting sands
Of relativity, indeterminacy, and impermanence.
Where is the rock upon which truth rests?
Can it be found in the external world?
Does it rest within some internal, intuitive awareness
That transcends all conditional states?
Or is truth only a phantom, an illusion, an unfulfilled hope?

The Irrationality of the Rational

We all put great faith in the rational
As products of a scientific age.
The world is seen as linear, logical, and controllable.
Decision making is objective and rational.
The irrationality of the rational is not questioned.
Four basic beliefs underlie this rationality.
First, the material world is primary.
(How was this material originated?)
Second, thought is based on brain function.
(Or is brain function based on thought?)
Third, all causation occurs in the physical.
(If it does not occur there, it does not exist.)
(Thought itself, however, is nonmaterial.)
Fourth, the physical world arose without cause.
(What caused the big bang?)
(Where was the matter before the big bang?)
(Where did this matter come from?)
All four of these beliefs are irrational, i.e.,
They cannot be proven rationally.
This faith in unexamined rationality
Leads to many false beliefs
About reality and our basic nature.

The Power of Choice

The pursuit of personal power corrupts.
Pursuit of total personal power corrupts absolutely.
To gain the world and lose one's soul
Is the most-bitter lesson in life.
Yet, all seem destined to test this path.
Contrast Machiavelli and St. Francis of Assisi,
Hitler and Mother Theresa,
The princes of power and the Princes of Peace.
Every means to attain one's ends
In contrast to Love as the only means.
The means that is end in itself.
The world holds faith in Machiavelli,
The arms races, the endless conflicts,
We of little faith in the power of love.
What does it take to empower the world with love
Instead of destroy it with hate?
Can we learn to love the hated?
The powerful not for their power
But for their humility, compassion, and empathy?
There will never be Peace and Joy
Without our total commitment to love.

Stress

The world seems full of stress.
Derived from every need addressed.
Life appears a pressured mess.

Respect required for incompetent bosses.
Accept fate's dice the way they're tossed.
Shoulder each apparent new loss.

The way the world appears to run
Life seems a bittersweet pun,
With only fleeting room for laughter and fun.

Is it possible to suppose
The world really does not impose
Stress; it's only a thought that arose?

Belief is all you really know.
Believe it; that makes it so.
Ideas from the mind outward flow.

Control resides within the mind,
Selective perceptions of every kind,
Confirm the kind of world you find.

Control of the mind resides with you.
Stress reflects mind's selective view.
Thoughts require close review.

What you think is real to you.
Thoughts determine how you feel.

Let peace be the thought your mind reveals.

Believe in love, wherein peace resides,
Project it outward from the mind,
Find a world were love no longer hides.

Is This All There Is?

Nothing is mine; I only use it for a while.
The house I live in, for others soon.
The air I breathe, shared by all.
The light follows darkness defines each day.
Each season succeeds as years proceed.
The baby dies as the man ascends.
The young each year the old become.
The birth of one, death balances.
Life replaced by life, a constant sum.
Nothing here that's mine lasts for long.
Is there more to life than this?
What persists; what belongs to me?
Do I have an eternal home someplace,
Diminished for none?
Where darkness never follows the light.
Where love is all there is.
Where mind's alive and never dies.
Where age and immortality are one.

Attachment

We have a thousand things around the house,
And every time I go to throw one out
The past reaches out and holds me fast.

I know the memories are mine alone,
And when I'm gone, this treasure trove
Will be viewed as junk and easily thrown.

Strange how inanimate things elicit the past,
Distorted now, but yet still alive,
With emotional attachments that won't die.

It's really quite a present burden,
Not just the things that clutter the house,
But the memories that channel the mind,

Limiting the present potential of self
To perceptions compatible with who I was,
Tied to personal history, self-imposed.

Oh to be completely unbound and free!
The unlimited Spirit God created me.
Throw out the past; live only in the now.

But in the present, I'm burden bound
By memories that fill my head,
Creating a self-image I built instead.

Life Force

Not gravity's force or entropy's pull
Propels life on its destined course.
Gene with gene combine
To unleash life's force in every cell,
Organized, dynamic, beyond any simple sum,
Resplendent diversity in love begun.

Each life event reveals new lessons
Of deep wisdom, indwelling.
At every turn, the onward rush impels
New soul vistas that enhance the self,
'Til death's stillness quiets the quest.
Soon a new cycle begins:
Nothing lost, just renewed again.

Life

Life is a spiritual exercise
Where no pain no gain prevails.
From comfort comes little spiritual push
To divest perception of its state of current arrest.
No questioning, no doubt, no discomfort, no despair,
No urge for higher ground to be aware.
If all is well in the world we make,
There is no work for us to undertake.
But traumas in life fall like unexpected rain,
And in each trauma's aftermath,
A need exists to rebuild beliefs.
Some perceptions remain unchanged,
While others expand to meet the new demands
To adequately explain the pain.
Not dikes against a flood,
But arks to glide on life's quick tide
To reach safe harbor on the other side,
Where only love resides.
Life's sea extends from birth to death,
Its turbulent storms contrast
With the inner peace that caulks the leaks,
As each ark sails for life's far shore.
Not one ark alone, but a whole fleet,
Spread across life's ocean swells
In wave trough and peak,
All riding a single sea,
Common journey, homeward bound.

Death's Lesson

Death so capricious,
What meaning can life have?
Death so uncontrolled,
What does one feel
About life and death?
Is fear all that's left?
Can death be real
If God is Love?
If death is the end,
Then there's only despair.

The Spiral Staircase

Life is a spiral staircase of spiritual development.
Each step affords a new and different view.
Not just higher with each step ascended,
But a new and different twist is added too.
Many landings break the ascent on which to rest,
On some for weeks, others months or even years.
Extra desire required to leave security behind.
Intuitively, somehow, the time to move is known.
The pleasure of understanding from looking back
Pushes spirit ever upward the spiraling course ahead.
Every new perception gained, leading to a higher plain,
Some at such dizzying heights, others content to stay
At lower levels and play ego games along the way.

The Dragon

The dragon we all have to slay
Resides with us each waking day.
It was born and grew along with us,
As each cultural block was laid, and thus,
To know fully who we really are
Requires we untangle our cultural snarl.

The dragon is such a fiery beast,
Our attention on him does solely feast.
He focuses almost all our thoughts
On fear, anger, and battles fought.
Until he is finally laid to rest,
To the real Self we cannot attest.

Our cultural self or ego being
Is all that most of us are seeing.
But when this beast is known as illusion,
Our spiritual being emerges devoid of confusion.
This inner knowing is quiet and calm,
In contrast to the dragon's states of alarm.

To slay the dragon at our gate,
Recognize we're not masters of our fate.
Renounce the control we never had;
Belief in it is only a cultural fad.
Rejoice in knowing God's not dead,
But is the life force guiding each of us instead.

Did we create ourselves? Just ask.
Choose our birth or this life's mask?

Perhaps we know just when and how we shall die,
Or choose the place in life we presently occupy.
Can all this be by chance mutation?
Or is man an integral part of God's creation?

We must transcend our culture's scientific myopia
To achieve the spiritual awareness that is our utopia.
Only then, will the dragon breathing fire at our gate
Be slain to reveal our true, natural state,
United with God, not separate in the world our thoughts make.
The universal love of all, by each, is what it takes.

The world of which we are all a part
Was made by God from the very start.
As God made the world, so man was made.
Let the unity of this knowing never fade.
God's creation of man in the world as One,
The cloth from a single spiritual thread was spun.

Culture's Mask

Culture molds, controls
In multitudinous
Gross and subtle ways
Until we hardly know
Where culture leaves off
And the I begins.

Perhaps the only I
We know
Is the cultural self.
Some say the ego
Is the only self;
Others disagree.

To transcend culture
And unmask True Self,
No little task,
Achieved by few.
The ecstatic view,
So humbling vast.

The Occident, the Orient, and the Mystical

Each culture indoctrinates its own kind,
Creating seeming differences across cultural lines,
No greater than between Occident and Orient.
One values group identity and responsibility,
The other the individual over the group,
Apparent irreconcilable divides.

The mystical asserts we are all one.
Separateness is only an illusion of the ego,
Everyone and everything a manifestation of God.
Cultural differences reinforce the ego but not the Self.
Love, compassion, cooperation, oneness, the universal condition,
Cultural differences only an illusion of separateness.

One world, room only for Oneness,
One humanity, united by its creation,
Living in mutual cooperation and harmony,
Not judging by the illusions of appearances
But loving in the knowledge
All are one in the unity of the Divine.

What Am I?

For sixty years, I've been asking the wrong question.
But then, I've been a slow learner.

Caught up in wondering who I am, I was lost in an ego maze of blind alleys,

Unaware that from above, a maze is easily solved.
To rise above the walls, a change in perception is needed.

A shift from who am I to what am I severs the preoccupation with personal history.

It focuses instead on concerns about the nature of one's existence.

Am I, as science suggests, just temporal and biochemical, or am I Ever AM, spiritual and eternal.

From higher ground, the maze the ego made is seen as interesting but no longer profound, confining, or confounding.

Fame

Fame is a fatal attraction,
A seductive illusion,
Pursued by the ego
In an attempt
To grasp immortality.
Yet in this pursuit,
It strangely affirms mortality
By trying to persist beyond
The demise of the physical body.

Identifying with the body
While trying to avoid its end,
The ego controls life's goals,
Strengthens its power,
And creates the illusion
That immortality is possible in this world,
Where nothing is permanent.

Immortality is only of the spirit.
It already is the nature of our being,
Beyond any effort or affect of the ego.
Attraction to personal fame
Is the ego's way of reinforcing the reality
Of the physical body and the fear of death,
Denying our spiritual existence.

Sometimes fame is an accident,
Unsought by the ego,
Derived from helping others.
When fame is not an ego goal,

The self becomes lost in a larger identity.
Fame becomes insignificant, unintended,
A part of universal brotherly love.
Only love, not fame, is everlasting,
Because only love God understands.

The Dream

Life's contrasts stand juxtaposed,
The birth of Cindy, the death of Rose,
Life's joys and sadness imposed.

Victory's triumph, defeat's despair,
Wealth's abundance, poverty's snare,
Fate's lot without a seeming care.

Most careful plans to no avail.
The terrorist bombs by fate prevail.
Are dualities all that life entails?

The daily paper confirms in its columns
News events both joyous and solemn,
Time recording each as it unfolds.

Is this the only way to know this world?
Can perception change so we might know
Love and release death's fearful hold?

This change will not be in the papers,
Rather seek deep within
To find love's eternal splendor.

Changed perception of freedom,
Life's dualities unified by Love,
Soul's light in the darkest night.

Death only appears to exist,
Only Love persists,
Awakened meaning, the ego resists.

The Journey

Welcome, courageous pilgrim,
The journey has begun,
So much to learn, embrace, affirm.
Keep the map close at hand,
Don't lose sight of the master plan.
Let the heart be the compass that lights the way
Through this fog-enshrouded stay.

Inner knowledge plots the course,
Invisible hands at the wheel.
Known yet unknown, concealed yet revealed,
Often circuitous, sometimes pained,
Always learning, never quite explained,
Famous and infamous all the same.
Time seems short for the task at hand,
Create only in love, the Captain's one command.

This Me

Who is this me I constantly see
Projected outward and reflected back to me?
Never a thought totally free,
So captured by self-enrapture.
An onion of concentric rings,
Covering layer on layer the wellsprings
Of creation's core where spirit soars.

Peel each layer as courage dares,
Experience freedom as each is pared.
Remove forever the shifting fear.
Release the "truths" held so dear.
Restrained by nothing, all removed,
The shining light no longer dimmed
By ego shadows cast,
The Self, at last, unmasked.

Shrouds and Veils

Shrouds and veils are symbols for the concealment
Of the great mystery underlying life, self, and death.
The conscious mind shrouds the unconscious.
Dreams veil the unconscious in symbols.
How do we penetrate to the core of being
To understand the meaning of life, self, and death?
Fame, wealth, glory, power, and many other goals
Veil life's true meaning by their seductive power.
The personas assumed in pursuit of these goals
Veil our true being in acts of endless doing.
We are all actors on a false stage of veiled life and being,
Awaiting the shrouded mystery of death.
Where is that detached, objective awareness
Needed to pierce the veils revealing life's true value?
Seek within, and you shall find.

Understanding Judas

Within each a potential Judas lives.
Deny it and we deceive ourselves,
Believing instead we are supermen.

If betrayal is a mortal sin
Punished by eternal damnation,
As the Bible seems to state,

God help us then,
We mortal men, for
From Judas we all descend.

It makes no sense
To think this way,
Since God is love and nothing more.

Punishment is not part of love,
It therefore does not exist
Within the mind of God.

Punishment is made by guilt
Within the minds of men,
Dispensed by eager, earthbound hands.

Oh Canada

Emotional joy welled up and grew,
As thousands of snow geese flew,
Creation's presence revealed anew.
Surrounded by the whir of wings,
Lost is the I of separate things
In a moment of Eternal awareness.

Tears of joy fill the eye,
As endless lakes to the horizon lie,
Reflecting the sunset's final sigh.
So grand a scale confounds the me,
It expands beyond what senses see,
Feeling only joy revealed in Thee.

White mountain bosoms pierced
By rock granite spires
Inspire beyond knowing,
Self-identity reeling,
Awakens a spiritual sense
Of Creation's eternal bliss.

Nature's Gift

Sometimes it takes nature's unique grandeur
 to momentarily transcend ordinary perception,
Healing the separation of knower and known:
An at-one-ment with all creation,
 a unity of creation and creator.

This total awareness comes without anticipation,
 a complete unthinking absorption.
Total engagement in the beauty,
 the magnitude, the miraculous fathomless.

The Virtues of Life

Flowers' beauty celebrate
The limitless bounty of life.
Who can be poor when beauty abounds?

A birth extends love in life,
Revealing our true nature.
Who can be weak united in love?

Laugher heals separation.
Humor cements our common bond.
Who can laugh and be alone?

Work creates abundance,
An expression of love in action.
Who can create scarcity by working?

Forgiveness is love extended,
The self and other as one.
Who can ever be alone again?

Among Many

A Universe so vast the
Mind reels to comprehend.
Arrogance and ignorance
Suggest we are alone.
More stars than grains of sand
On all the beaches of this world,
Alone we still believe.
From mountaintop to ocean depth,
Life thrives, adapts, expands:
Unique, we still imagine.
From tribe and clan
To town and nation-state,
Mind remains confined.
Despite escape to outer space,
Alone we still insist.
The solar system no longer unique,
Others known to exist.
What will it take to free the mind
To grasp creation's grandeur?
How long can we persist
In this arrogant belief
That man is separate and unique?
Know we are not alone,
Just part of the wholeness
Of God's magnificent Creation.

A World to Choose

Plato said it two thousand years ago,
So all who follow might clearly know:
Sense perceptions are mind shadows on the wall,
Distorted replicas of ideas; that is all.

We create our world of reality,
Fully believing it's out there to see.
Seeing is believing, we all know,
Whereas "believing is seeing" is more apropos.

Jesus said heaven is to be found within.
So close your eyes and let real knowing in.
The sensory world is a pleasant illusion.
Be not deceived by its seductive confusion.

Focus instead on the reality of mind
That binds all of us together as one mankind.
The mind we share with God and each other
Is there for each of us to discover.

Allow yourself to look beyond the senses,
To a realization of Being devoid of pretenses.
A Oneness of Love without any limit,
Awareness affirms our belief in it.

Let the Peace that flows from this understanding
Embrace us all, the hostile world not withstanding.
In God all together, both you and me,
Extend Love and Peace to all, eternally.

Are We Ready?

It has been said that power corrupts,
And total power corrupts completely.
But before the power were the needs of the ego,
And ego needs are endless.
Power is the means of satisfying ego desires.
Where is the philosopher king of Plato's *Republic*,
A person of wisdom, compassion, and humility?
Would we elect a Christ or a Buddha?
We get what our level of collective awareness demands.
Will elections reveal our higher self,
Or only the ego needs of which we are all too familiar?

Life's True Story

Every life is a unique story,
yet surprisingly, all the same.
Physically each is different;
even identical twins
differ slightly in some ways.
Mental and emotional differences
often seem profound.

Body, mind, soul, spirit,
only at the ego level
are differences found.
Identify with the body or mind,
and differences between
self and others are seen.

Identify with soul (Self),
and differences disappear
until, in pure Spirit,
there is only the Divine One.

Contradictions on the Spiritual Path

Life is a spiritual journey;
Humanity as a whole is on a path,
As is each individual.
The Bible, along with many other books,
Records humanity's collective journey.
Biblical contradictions are road markers,
Where significant transformations
Of consciousness have occurred.
An eye for an eye, to turn the other cheek,
A judging and punishing to a loving God,
A local to a universal Deity,
A God without to a Spirit within.
Individuals may use these travel logs
To facilitate their own spiritual development.
They are only guides, however, not *your* journey.
Humanity as a whole is on a slow track.
The individual may choose his/her own pace.
Using the record of collective consciousness,
The individual may personally surge ahead
Or lag behind until roused from slumber.
Biblical contradictions are milestones,
Marking humanity's progress.
Recognize your own individual contradictions
As opportunities for personal, spiritual transformation.

Art and Creativity

The creative act of the artist
Comes from the unknown into the known.
Artistic skill is the vehicle of manifestation,
Expressing life, yet life-transcending.
Each media, each method, is a partial representation
Of the harmony, beauty, and oneness
Struggling to be found in life.
Through each individual's unique experience,
Artistic expression builds a bridge to shared unity.
Different art forms and different artists
Appeal differently to various people
Based on shared life experiences.
But beyond these individual idiosyncrasies,
The universal must be present to be art,
Otherwise it is just another sensory manifestation,
Devoid of true creative expression.
Art is a window on the universal,
Buried deep within the human psyche.

Beauty

Beauty may be in the eye of the beholder.
Like the rainbow created by a prism,
Perception of beauty is formed
By the culture surrounding the beholder.
This beauty is limited and transitory,
Unconsciously accepted as real,
A "reality" narrowed into the contemporary.

Beauty dances across the screen of life,
Dependent on cultural blinders.
Satisfied with a restricted self,
Afraid of unconditional grandeur,
We lack the wisdom to see
What is truly beautiful.
Can we ever know?

Creativity

Creativity, originality, spontaneity, improvisation, inspiration,
Where do they come from, the mind, spirit, beyond self?
In the arts, music, literature, science, sports, are they all the same?
The great unmanifest awaiting manifestation,
The unknown future arriving in the present.
What are the limits of human potential?

In Diversity One

My fingerprint upon this page
Is uniquely mine.
Just as each person's life
Contributes to
The human race.

Never underestimate your worth.
Mankind depends on you.
Within the web of life,
Each woven strand adds strength
To the fabric's total might.

This earth and all who live here,
From one source are derived.
The external diversity
Of our uniqueness only hides
The unity that within All resides.

Arrogance

Twenty-two years of solitary.
Retained in an enclosed pen.
No contact with fellow beings.
Confined, no longer free,
The crime? Being nonhuman.
The sentence? Imprisonment for life.
A slave, required to perform for supper.
No contact with its pod.
How does a dolphin feel?
Bored? Sad? Depressed? Mad?
To whom is there an appeal?
Is man's arrogance ever to be healed?

The Zoo

A zoo is the ultimate in human arrogance.
If elephants cry, and observers say they do,
Should such sensitive beings be held captive in a zoo
To entertain and educate those who come to view?

We call ourselves human, but in the way we behave,
There is little humanity in our condescending, superior stance.
Preservation, we say, makes captivity needed,
But shouldn't it be in forest or plain and not the zoo?

Estimating

When I was young, I thought I'd never die.
Now, near seventy-five, death seems more neigh.
Very young, I didn't estimate at all,
Took what came, reveling in the joy of life.
Maybe Christmas started time estimates first.
From now to Christmas stretched to infinity.
Then summer vacation an eon away.
Adolescence, becoming an adult, half a light-year removed.
Now time seems only short, not enough, despite less to do.
Sometimes time seems to disappear.
Nothing to estimate; it simply isn't there.
Estimating time a relative skill,
Is there a time that's really true?

Home

Where is the place for me to be at home?
Is home a place or a state of mind?
Maybe both: a place associated with a mental state.
Can that state make any place a home?

Maybe home's neither place nor state of mind,
But anywhere kindred spirits find
Companionship of the heartfelt kind.
Relationships make a home, regardless of where people roam.

Nomad's tent, itinerant farmer's shack, trailer park,
Penthouse, tenement slum, motor home,
Victorian mansion, log cabin, adobe hut,
Houseboat, barge, junk, tepee, igloo, castle.

Each is different, yet all are the same,
Places of deep emotional commitment,
The sharing that gives life meaning:
Everywhere is the heart at home.

How Long?

Each hilltop castle capped,
Every town a wall surrounds,
With towered gate and drawbridged moat,
Defense against all those without,
Unrecognized as fellow men.

Fields grow silos underground,
With restless missiles poised
To thunder in defense's name
And kill and maim all those
Unrecognized as fellow men.

Fear's cycle endlessly extends,
Unaltered now, as then.
What does it take to break its hold
And free the human mind
To know all as fellow men.

Into the Next Decade

As one moves into decade number eight,
We give thanks for being here so long
And remember others now long gone.
The love we've shared, the pain we've known,
The mistakes we've made, the way we've grown.
Life just as mysterious now as ever before,
Still time to wonder and explore.
Eternity stands still in the ever now.
The body certainly not the same,
Yet buried deep within, the soul remains
Unchanged now as it was then.
The path leads onward without end.

Thought Changes the World

Normally we think technology,
Rooted in external reality,
As man's instrument for change.
It is merely an implemented idea.
It seems real, because it is observed externally.
Contemplate Love, Compassion, Divinity,
Immortality, Interdependence,
Joy, Peace, Perfection, and Bliss.
Realization of these inner states
Creates the basis of our perception of
External reality greater than
Any technological impact.
The external is a projection of the internal.
Mind, or thought, comes first,
External reality follows.
The power of sense perception
To define external reality
Is merely a collective myth,
Created by the power of the mind.
Mind gives meaning to everything that is perceived.

Map or Territory?

Life is the territory;
The computer screen the map.
We've had lots of maps:
Photographs, radio,
The movie screen,
Later came television,
Now the Internet.
Life is relationship,
The computer simulation.
Life is personal contact,
The computer a machine,
Three-dimensional reality
On a flat screen.
Soon, virtual reality
Replacing a walk in the woods.
Can humanity cope with this flight into semi-reality?
Human contact mediated by machine.
Map and territory ever more blurred.

Marriage

Two separate paths from different pasts
Merge today to wind its way
Into shadows the future casts.
Sunlit, washed by rain,
Up steep hills, past snow-capped peaks,
Around sharp curves, across rivers wide,
At sunset, the glistening sea is reached,
Journey's end, a time to rest.

Renewal is life's endless cycle.
From different families each has come
To a new life here begun.
Today's commitment starts
A union greater than its parts.
A troth to each other but something more,
A new generation begins
With the family these two have become.

Let unconditional Love
Be the abiding goal,
Found in forgiveness
Of self and each other.
With only Love to give
Only Joy is known,
Where Peace abides
As love is sewn.

Let love light life's path,
Dispersing shadows adversity casts.
Guiding these travelers

Past pitfalls and traps,
To the safe haven of inner peace
That unconditional love creates,
Growing to embrace
The whole human race.

A New Journey Begins

It's Christmas time again,
Another year almost gone.
But Zack is here,
And the special year
Extends and extends.
New life begins
To be fulfilled.

Each new birth
New hope promised,
Like the one
Twenty centuries ago.
Love's bonds renewed,
Rededicated soul,
The search renewed.

Each newly Divine
Being must find
The way home.
Found by love
For everyone,
Yet each a special case,
That seems unique, alone.

Yet bonded all
In life's travail
By birth and death
The transcendent points
That light the path.
True knowledge waits
In life entwined.

Off the Deep End

Common wisdom dictates, “Don’t go off the deep end.”
Do not lose your mind. Be rational. Think logically.
This is the consciousness of the external world of the senses.
The inner-world of Self-experiencing is, “Off the deep end.”
To lose your mind is to find your Self.
The world of things and doing needs your mind, your ego self;
The world of being needs only witnessing awareness.
Meditation is diving off the deep end.

The Mantra

The ego makes a lock
For perception's door
That blocks the way
To our true Self.

Each of us makes
Our own individual lock,
So each must find
Our own personal key.

But some masters
Have found a master key
That many can use
To unlock their door.

Breath in, relax
Breath out, smile
Breath in, Now is the perfect
Breath out, moment.

Why is this mantra a master key?
Because it requires
No intellectual belief in it.
All you have to do is do it.

Relax: the in-breath itself
Is totally relaxing.
The stomach muscles relax,
As the diaphragm drops.

You cannot be relaxed
And fearful at the same time.
Fear is the absence of love.
If you are totally relaxed, you are in a state of love.

Smile: the out-breath disseminates your smile,
Communicating the Joy of being at peace.
A smile creates a physiological state of peace.
You cannot smile and be angry at the same time.

Now is the perfect moment; there is nothing else.
Time is a function of ego fantasy.
Can the world's religions
Agree on what year it is?

Meditation

At first, the mantra "Ever AM"
Seemed to mean I live forever.
Later, "Ever Am" was identified
As an all-powerful, external God.
Then, "Ever Am" became the God within.
Now it seems to be the suchness
Of awareness: the eternal now.
The knower separate from I,
Yet somehow the Me
That is not me.
That same witness
There as a child,
Present now,
Unchanging "Ever Am."

A Helping Hand

We all know helping others is "good."
But what does this really mean?
Surely not having others do
What we, "know is best for them."
You are your brother's keeper
But what should we do?
Perhaps what we do doesn't matter.
It's the spirit of doing that counts.
Involvement without attachment
Is the recommendation of the East.
Loving without judgment
The message from the West.
In different ways, both seem to say
The outcome IS the process.
The act of loving generates itself.
Only the ego is concerned with results
And becomes entangled in endless means
Judged to be related to different outcomes.
But the act and outcome are the same,
Because any means can be an expression of love.
Since only the love is real, the means don't matter.
Believe in love, act in love, be love.
We become not only our brother's keeper
But our own as well.
The outcome is assured.

Only Love Extends

Some people think that fear is real;
Believing makes it true for them.
But love is all there really is
And has no opposite at all.

Fear of being rebuffed or rejected,
Forgetting that only love extends,
Makes defensiveness our state,
Separating us from them.

If love is all we see,
Then reaching out's a joy,
Confirming in each relationship
The love we knew we'd find.

The world forever changed
By each simple act of love.
No different than it ever was,
Just relearned and taught anew.

The Dance of Life

In the beginning, a rocking lullaby,
Then early childhood's frantic jig,
Adolescence's rebellious rock and roll,
Adult's tangos, foxtrots, rumbas;
For others, the swaying blues.
Graduation and wedding marches,
Quiet minuets, ballets, and waltzes,
A chorus of nostalgic songs
Place markers of time's passage.
In the end, the pallbearer's
Cadenced step; for some, Dixieland.

On the Death of a Friend

Can it be true?
It seems unreal.
So near and dear,
Now gone to stay.

The odds so good,
Or so they said.
But then, those odds
Weren't meant for you.

So young, so alive,
So needed, so loved,
How can it be true?
What's now to be done?

Life must have meaning.
Is it for us to know?
Its measure of deeds and years
So meaningless against the tears.

Unknowing

This place of
Fear and pain.
Death everywhere,
Is there
No place
To escape?
A little peace
A moment's love
Sharp contrast
Against the
Waiting abyss.
What hope
Is there
To find
A way
To make
Life real,
Know truth,
Feel secure,
Live life
Completely free
Of fear
And pain?
No hope
At all
If one
Believes
The body
Is all
And Spirit

Is dead.
We who
Are so
Holy know
Not who
We are.

Never Apart

In times of joy and those of tears,
The passing days, months, years,
You are near.
The baby's birth, the parent's death,
The graduate's celebration,
You are here.
In marriage vows, separations, and divorce,
In work's demands and vacation fun,
Your presence always known.
The circle expands and then contracts,
As friends appear and then depart,
You're still here.
The life force ebbs and flows,
Sickness, health, joy, despair,
Your love is always there.
There is no separation, despite how life appears.
Enfolded in your embrace,
Life's force is love. Celebrate!
It never ends.
It never starts.
It ever is.
It is you!

Playmate

When I was seven, eight, and nine,
Every day I played with a friend of mine;
His name was I. L. Thomas, as I recall.
Mostly we'd pretend we were soldiers fighting a war
That not too long before, our dads had fought and won.
An old gas mask, steel helmet, and wooden guns our props.
In sandy soil an entrenchment dug,
Covered with boards, old tin ceiling sheets, then dirt.
This backyard redoubt captured, lost, recaptured again,
An endless fantasy fight between the best of friends.
Then one day he moved away, and like an armistice,
It all came to an abrupt end, my loss, a friend.
I often wonder what happened to him and other playmates, too.
So important in one's life for a while,
Then gone, only a farewell smile,
The permanent separation unrealized then.
Some would say they've never really gone away,
So long as memories stay.
We played so hard at this game of war,
Every day for those several years.
Considering what was about to come,
Was this some sort of precognitive fear,
Through play, being prepared for the future?
Maybe that steel helmet and gas mask, real tools of war,
Were too powerful psychometric objects for the minds of boys?
Or were we two World War One soldiers reincarnated,
Gaining control over the uncontrollable in a previous life.
Absurd? No less so than life's personal journey,
Deep, meaningful, powerful, emotional relationships,
Tomorrow, gone, back into the void from which they came.
How do you understand it: chance, or is there some plan?

Optimism

Where does it come from,
The optimism of the young?
Why is it so often gone
By age sixty-five?
Cynicism like a cancer
Seems to grow with age,
An unwelcome companion
Of life's traumatic events.

The loss of faith
In human goodness
A cause perhaps
Of the cynical view.
Too much exposure to
Greed, aggression,
Suffering, and
Uncaring self-interest.

But what of those
Whose optimism is undimmed?
Altruists to the end,
Exposed to life's traumas, too,
But immune to cynicism,
Vaccinated by love,
Giving, caring, forgiving,
Still young and alive at sixty-five.

Serendipity and Creativity

Serendipitous creativity is escape
From self-imposed limitations we make.
Spirit is ever boundless and free.
Within time and culture, we accept limitations.
Serendipity happens when we
Perceive from the larger, boundless Self.
Creatively we reorganize perceptions
Beyond usually agreed-upon limits,
Relating the new insight
To the old, now new, paradigm.
Thus is the true Self
Continuously revealed.

The Barge Ride

The two-mule team
Stretches the towrope tight,
The barge begins to move
In smooth silence at a walking pace,
The treelined banks ease by.
Mind recalls the leisure pace,
One hundred fifty years melt away,
Another place, another time,
A different life regained.

In the woods beyond the bank,
A steam train backs down a rusty track,
Replacement for the mule-towed barge.
Noisy, dirty, bumpy, fast,
End of the leisure tranquil past.
Soon to be replaced
By truck and motorcar.
The airplane now compresses time,
Shrinks distances beyond barge rider's minds.

The space port on the horizon looms,
Foreshadowing a new culture's reach
Beyond the Earth, Moon, Planets, Sun,
Into the emptiness of outer space,
Recapturing at speeds beyond belief
The quiet tranquility of silent space.
Two hundred years of technology's march,
Yet the need for inner tranquility remains
Whatever the society's external pace.

The Civil War

The battlefields are immortalized as National Parks,
Commemorating those who died in the slaughter
To save the Union or preserve their way of life.
From the perspective of almost 150 years,
How do we understand this most horrible war?
Can humankind only resolve its differences by combat?
Is "might makes right" our only method of last resort?
Surely there must be a better way.
Yet, we still continue an endless series
Of conflict resolutions by war.
Those who pay the ultimate price,
Remembered for their sacrifice,
But what a horrific price to benefit others.
Common sense dictates a more humane solution.
When will humanity climb out of the valley of death
To new heights of Love, Joy, and Peace,
No longer demanding the sacrifice of death
To demonstrate humanity's interdependent Oneness?

Friendly Fire

Thomas "Stonewall" Jackson, Confederate general in the Civil War,
Was killed by his own troops while on nighttime reconnaissance.
Every war results in "unintended" killings,
Friendly fire, collateral damage, civilian casualties, accidents.
Fear, anger, and confusion the cause.

If humanity is part of the seamless Divine Creation,
Isn't all killing friendly fire from the spiritual perspective?
"Do no harm," a spiritual level we have not yet attained,
The miraculous Oneness of Creation still beyond realization.
Let us be aware and live in our state of AT-ONE-MENT.

Inside Out

Somewhere out there, we think we'll find
The perfect place to create peace of mind.
Perhaps the surf's murmured roar
Will create a state that lets Spirit soar.
Maybe the quiet of the desert's vast expanse
Will allow inner knowing to advance.
The grandeur of a white-capped mountain peak
Perhaps speaks to the Infinite others seek.
But in truth, we're never alone.
Spirit always abides deep within.
No special place is ever required
To find the Source to which we aspire.
God is here, there, everywhere we are;
No need to chase after some distant place.
Deep within, a quiet Spirit sleeps,
Needing only loving desire,
To give It the internal space
All seek, but few embrace.

Awake

Asleep, Awake, Enlightened

Most of humanity sleeps,
Some are awake,
Very few enlightened.
Thinking leads to understanding,
The rational, the thinking mind.
Awareness of the thinking
Begins the awareness of being.
Who is aware of the thinking?
Non-thinking, naked awareness,
Reveals pure Being.
The known and knower one.
Meditation the bridge
From awake to enlightened.

Immortal One

Loving, learning, growing, yearning,
Extolling, neglecting, embracing, rejecting,
Always different, yet still the same.

Looking, finding, losing, hiding,
Believing, revealing, recalling, forgetting,
Ever changing, yet unchanged.

Knowing, erring, moving, staying,
Living, dying, laughing, crying,
Fleeting now, yet everlasting.

Peaceful, tranquil, ever known,
At rest, secure, eternally at home,
By life unmasked, in each enthroned.

One Thing to Learn

There is only one thing we all must learn.
We already know it anyway,
But in the mind, it seems not to stay.
God and man are One.

We did not create ourselves.
Only the ego was made by us.
Each perceived as separate,
Thus concealing our true reality in diversity.

Since God and man are One,
Man, like God, has limitless power.
The misperceptions we make tower
Over the quiet truth of inner knowing.

Collectively, we deceive each other,
Believing each a separate being,
Competing in the world we are creating,
An illusion so powerful we can't escape.

To know that man and God are One,
Is a powerful, new perspective,
Permitting the healing corrective,
That separation alone allows for enemies.

If I am you, and you are me, by our God identity,
Then my forgiving you is really my forgiving me.
Forgiveness, in love, transcends our separate reality,
Confirming instead our Universal Being.

If all of us are spiritually a single One,
Most of what we believe about the world
Is clearly without foundation and absurd,
Testimony to the power of our collective misperception.

Life Center

Here at the center, I ever am,
Quietly at peace and serene.
While all around me
A tumultuous world
Swirls, whirls, and twirls.
Like the hurricane's eye am I.

Awareness

What is this
Unchanging presentness?
Unseen, but seeing,
Unheard, but hearing,
Unaffected, yet feeling,
Detached, yet belonging,
Conscious, yet beyond mind,
Witness, experiencer,
Awareness beyond I-ness,
Self of the self,
Unchanging Love
Ever manifesting.

A Broader Horizon

Heredity versus environment,
Preoccupation of biology and psychology
For over one hundred years.
Environment focuses on the external,
Heredity on the internal,
Seemingly unalterable for humans until now.
Is it time for change?
Will attention shift to the interaction
Of mind, body, and spirit,
An expanded dynamic
Redefining the individual?
What are the limits?
What is the potential?
We hardly know.
Awaken the sleeping giant
Of our full capacity.
Live beyond our physical limits.
Discover all we already are.
Old, limited controversies
Fade into insignificance.

Thickening Smoke Screen

Like a little destroyer darting about,
Concealing the fleet from enemy eyes,
The ego's profuse verbiage and intricate ideas
Mask the profound truth to which spirit aspires.
Within this smoke screen of ideation, the Self quietly hides.

Distracted, confused by what was intended to be saved,
Light dims for all those trapped within
This self-made stultifying haze.
The only solution seems to be
More protection, more smoke, reducing what we see.
If we need to be saved from our belief in death,
Blindly groping in this intellectual haze
Seems a small price to be paid.
We're unaware of the light surrounding
The intellectual fog the ego has made.

Suppose there is no enemy against which to defend,
Only immortality awaits, without end.
The fresh breeze of new understanding
Clears the ego's smoke screen away,
Self, in bright enlightenment bathed.

We of Misplaced Faith

Oh we of misplaced faith
Who see ourselves
As frail and weak,
Vulnerable to death's
Every beck and call.
Awake to know
Your loving self,
Created in the
Mind of God,
Extending His Creation
To one and all.
The love that
Sees no other
Finds only Oneness
Instead of separation.
Be home at last
In love's brilliant light
That casts
No shadow anywhere.

A Zero-Sum Game

Most of us believe life is a zero-sum game.
My gain your loss, birth balances death,
Nothing without its opposite.
Each set of opposites a balance whose sum is zero.
What if life were a sum of gains
Without opposites at all?
Hard to believe, given the evidence.
Look again beyond the appearance of opposites,
See the unity beyond the duality.
In the stock market, my loss or gain
Is independent of your gain or loss.
Even buying or selling the same stock,
You may have a loss or gain, but the price is the same.
Whatever the cost, it will be right for me.
When whales were killed for oil for lamps,
Other oil lay buried in the ground unfound,
Just an idea away from a whole new age.
No balance here: all new potential.
If material things are unbounded in this way,
Subject to the infinite potential of human mind,
Why do we still believe in the zero-sum game?
Because we identify with weakness, death, and littleness.
Our true potential lies beyond our wildest dreams.
Unlimited except by self-imposed
Negative and constrictive thoughts.
The power is with us.
Deep within we know.
Tap this endless source.
Go with its mighty flow!

The Rudderless Ship

The ego finds it hard to accept
That it steers through life
A rudderless ship.
So much in command
It fails to grasp
The unknown currents
Of life's sea.

Control on board
Enough for most.
Unknown departure
Or final port of call.
Sails trimmed,
Deck swabbed clean,
The tidy ship drifts on.

Beyond the rail
The great sea churns,
Uncontrolled by captain or crew.
Strong winds, high waves,
Deep currents
Mysteriously move
The rudderless ship.

Is it chance alone
That guides the ship?
Are these forces
Beyond the ship's control?
Or despite their appearance,
Are they part of some
Beneficent plan?

Is this soul ship
Safe on some unknown
Yet chosen course,
In harmony with
Some master plan?

The Non-Birthday Celebration

Celebrate the non-birth of Being.
Not the birth of the self you remember.
Before the mind was born, you were.
Before the body was born, you were.
After the mind is dead, you are.
After the body is dead, you are.
The past and future is of mind and body.
You are the eternal present.
Celebrate your eternal Self.

In the womb, you were, but mind was not.
Mind is only memory, and you don't recall.
Mind is the past, but you are now.
Mind is the future of your desires.
If mind is past and future,
Who is here now?
Celebrate the Being you know not.
The Self knows both life and death.
Know the Self and know your eternity.

Freedom and Slavery Then, Now, and Always

Freedom and slavery are opposite ends
Of the continuum of mindfulness.
Most think of slavery and freedom as external conditions.
In reality, they are internal states.
No person is free who is enslaved within.
No external enslavement can truly enslave
Where spiritual freedom enlightens the mind.
Jesus, who on the cross can say,
"Forgive them Father, for they know not what they do,"
Is a most powerful example of external enslavement
With the complete internal transformation of spiritual freedom.
Mindfulness or naked awareness is the path to freedom.
The thinking mind focused on the external is slavery.
The witness-self can unlock your prison cell,
Or you can remain forever enslaved by your thinking mind.

The Inner Path

Each grain of sand an unknown sun in creation's hand,
A universe so vast, beyond comprehension's grasp.
Walk all the shores of this world's seas,
An impossible task for you or me,
Too much for either of us to do or see.
Yet, all the sand grains passing under our feet,
Of more stars than these, is the universe replete.
Standing here upon the sand, halfway between,
The infinite expanse of the universe above,
And the subatomic immateriality of the beach,
The sand seems so firm; the only motion the wind and surf,
No discernable spin, no elliptical race, no explosive haste,
No sinking into the atomic space that constitutes materiality.
How easily the senses lie, on what can knowledge rely?
Science extends the senses by instruments and math's logic,
Describing a reality that defies ordinary reason,
Widening the gap between science and common experience.
Leaving most behind, with outmoded thinking,
Still groping to find answers to the meaning of existence
Based on the world revealed by our senses.
Does science help or hinder this task in a universe now so vast?
There is a smaller world to explore, much nearer.
Billions of neurons encased in bone,
Standing between the externally seen
And the internal flow only you can know.
Intricate structure, complex function mostly unknown,
The mystery of mind consciousness confounds
Its possessor with the ideas itself propounds.
Let vastness and complexity quiet the humble mind,
Sliding freely into the silence of inner peace,

Devoid of demands for rational thought,
A knowing beyond any sense deception,
An awareness of Self-revealing who we are,
Timeless, loving, unjudging, sure,
Confusion ended, old understanding restored.

Who's to Judge

At eighty-three, and death just days away,
He said, "As I look back on my life,
There is nothing that I would change."

Another, at age eighty-seven, said,
"I don't need to stay much longer.
I've done everything I wanted to do."

Neither of these men led perfect lives
As judged by others, like you and I,
Yet perfection lay in some grander eye.

Given all of life's vicissitudes,
How can there be at the end
This sense of completion without regret?

The Peace of SELF

In fear, I view the world
From my puny ego self,
Defense its major need.
Attack, defend, judge, assess:
Repeat the endless cycle again,
Fear reinforced anew
With death the ultimate end.

Choose Peace, Joy, and Love instead,
Grand message from the SELF.
Unheard, ignored, disbelieved,
Impossible in the world I see
Of separate selves in endless wars.
Learn how to know our SELF again
By choosing Peace not war.

Feel the Joy and Love
That comes from choosing Peace.
Feel the anger disappear,
As fear withers in Love's healing light.
The path you choose to take
Creates your Heaven or hell,
The difference your decision makes.

Practice choosing Peace
Each time you feel disturbed.
Tell yourself I choose Peace
Instead of anger and revenge.
Forgive yourself for being wrong,
Guilt only leads you further astray
From knowing who you really are.

Awaken to the SELF that's real,
Feel the Peace, the Love, the Joy.
There is no limit to your mind
To heal, just live the Peace
That radiates its quiet state,
Embracing all within its sheltered grace,
Where everyone finds their eternal place.

What to Do? Just Be

When a nation pursues the path of war,
What are the peace lovers to do?
If you know you are at One
With a loving, forgiving God,
Whose Peace and Joy passes all comprehension,
You only have to be what you know.
Doing increases opposition,
Reinforcing the fear, anger, and aggression
Of those advocating war.
Now they have you to hate too.
Be your true self.
Bear witness to love.
Fear not, there is no other.

A Peace of Mind

The search for Peace begins and ends within the mind.
It's not out there in the world to find.
Most think it's the world that forms the mind,
But the mind creates the world after its own kind.

If the world is formed by belief alone,
It can only confirm what's already known.
Discover the quiet wisdom inward sown.
Project it outward, so Peace in the world's at home.

Peace depends on love alone.
Forgive another, so little to atone.
Forsake throwing that first stone,
So Peace through love can be enthroned

The Great Mystery

The two great domains,
The material world
And the spirit,
One explored
By science
The other
By religion,
Now converging
On the One
Mysterious void.

Being Is not Doing

The ego self is doing.
The Self is being.
The ego thinks
There is no self
Without doing.
Death ends doing.
Who are you then?
You are Self.
The being
You always are
Before and after death,
The Divine self.

Meditation offers meaningless doing,
The transcendence of doing by repetition,
Allowing Being to emerge into awareness.
To know your Divine self you have nothing to do.
This is the hardest lesson, because it destroys the ego.
The ego thinks you are doing not being.
There is nothing wrong with doing;
Just don't confuse it with being.
Continue your identification with doing,
And you continue your ego identity.
Keep doing, but realize you are something more.
Stop doing, and allow yourself to discover Self.

The Chicken or the Egg?

Body, mind, spirit,
Brain, mind, soul,
A trinity that's one.
Scientists think like Descartes:
"I think, therefore I am."
The spiritualists believe
I am, therefore I think.
The scientists believe
The self is in the body.
The transcendentalists believe
The body is in the self.
The scientists believe
Consciousness is an epiphenomenon
Of the chemistry of the brain,
Changed by neural transmitters,
Endorphins, and psychedelic drugs.
Others believe consciousness
Precedes the materiality
Of the brain,
The brain merely
A channel of consciousness,
A transducer.
Scientists believe
Materiality is primary.
Spiritualists believe
Spirit is primary.
All these opposing
Dualistic views
In the end,
Must recognize

That all is one.
Creation is
A seamless whole,
And the Great Mystery
Can be looked at
Either way.

God or Goddess?

For the religions of the "Book,"
God is male, God the Father.
For the Greeks, Romans, and Hindus,
There are Gods and Goddesses.
The Goddess of Fertility reigned
For forty thousand years.
For the Deist and the Pantheist,
God is a sexless source or creator,
A nonanthropomorphic deity.
The Muslims and Buddhists
Believe that God is indefinable,
So no image is an adequate description.
Mohammed, Buddha, and Christ
Are spiritually enlightened teachers,
Thought of as Gods by some followers.
The S/He of Deity is as sexless as sunlight,
The sex a projection of a cultural time and place.

Anger

I get angry and think you made me so.
You're the one who caused, it I know.
Although the anger comes from me,
You're the source; it has to be!
If it were any other way, my fear would be revealed.
I'd much rather be angry than afraid,
Because fear is the source of this illusion that I've made.
Anger without fear cannot exist
Any more than illusion without fear can persist.
But what is the illusion that I must disbelieve
If I'm to be relieved of my fear and anger?
You are you, and I am me, each separate beings.
You are the source of the anger I'm feeling.
But fear and anger are not in the outside world.
They're thoughts inside my head instead.
Projecting fear and anger creates the illusion
That anger's source is outside myself.
The external world used to support my delusions.
But feelings arise within, where my responsibility begins.

Quiet the mind beyond perceived separation,
At-oneness in Peace and Love end all deception.
The world no longer perceived as insane,
Transformed into the wholeness of you and me, the same.

I Am, Therefore, I Think

Rene Descartes said,
"I think, therefore I am,"
Thus starting a four-hundred
Year focus on the
Epiphenomena of Being.

Better to have said,
"I am, therefore I think,"
Allowing for the penetration
Of the flow of consciousness
To the center of Being.

Who is it that is
Aware of the thinking?
A witness separate
From the thoughts,
Creator of thinking.

End of an Ice Age?

It was late in 1989 when the human thaw began.
Can it be the beginning of a new age for man?
The world so different now, shrunken as viewed from outer space,
Contracted by communication networks connecting every place,
A world economy that weakens the sovereignty of states,
A world traversed by contrails crisscrossing borderless airspace.
But how about the minds of men: are they still imprisoned?
Has the change affected all so a new era won't be forestalled?

The bigotries of race, religion, and nation are strong and deep.
Can man cut free the past, inhale the air freedom reaps?
Extend love with tolerance, forgiveness, responsibility, respect,
All part of one living whole, one earth, one people, one destiny.
Is it dream or reality, turning point or not?
Will this be the unifying of mankind's future lot?
Or are we destined never to unravel illusion's knot?

A 1999 New Year's Resolution for All

On the eve of a new decade,
The preamble of a new century,
The dawn of a new age,
Let us dedicate ourselves
To be only love.

If love is all we give,
Then love is all we know.
For giving is receiving,
In love, there is no "other";
Self is One in all.

Sunlight shines for everyone,
So love's warmth extends,
Reflected back again,
Continuing without end,
The circle that begins within.

Let the new age dawn,
Remembering we are
All sons and daughters of God,
United by love as one
Through forgiveness of all.

Let the realization dawn
That humanity has no limit
Within the oneness of God's creation.
God and we are only love,
There is no separation.

A Friend

One to count on 'til the end
For support, love, and defend
Your worth when others contend
You are less than God intends.

Love

Love all things in their season.
Not in the past or the future.
Love all things in the present.
Love and the present are all there is.

Life's Love Song

All ventures have the same refrain,
Love's challenge set in a new frame.
Place to place, person to person,
Job to job, it's all the same,
Open the heart to love's refrain.

Extend love's forgiving hand,
Love, life's call to all,
In love of others, our Self discovered.

Each new start, another song,
Every theme fits where it belongs,
Movements in life's symphony,
Counterpoint to strife's discord,
Harmonies that intone our destiny.

Extend love's forgiving hand,
Love, life's call to all,
In love of others, our Self discovered.

In the end, death finds us all,
But life's love song lingers on,
Each generation knows the tune,
Rewrites its themes to meet new dreams,
Until, in every land, all understand.

Extend love's forgiving hand,
Love, life's call to all,
In love of others, our Self discovered.

Can there be a more grand plan?
Universal love in every land,
Encircling the whole globe,
Each heart the start, none alone,
The world held in love's complete embrace.

Extend love's forgiving hand,
Love, life's call to all,
In love of others, our Self discovered.

Join love's chorus; wait no longer,
Be the one who makes love stronger,
You are the one to start the cycle,
Love expands with each forgiving,
Share the gift that ends despair.

Extend love's forgiving hand,
Love, life's call to all.
In love of others, our Self discovered.

Love's Promise

Let Love enlighten every heart,
So each fulfills their fated part
To free the mind of fear and greed,
Embraced by Love's eternal Grace.

May Love empower each thought and deed,
So brotherhood, that fertile seed,
Can crowd out bigotry and hate,
Released at last from fear's binding state.

Let Love shine forth in brilliant light,
Dispersing fear's long, shadowed night,
Transforming self into the All
Of quiet Peace and endless Bliss.

Love's Numerology

The real me is not the one you see.
The real me is the same as thee.
You, me, and God make three.
Or is it One that's all of me?
One, two, three, One,
It's all of us or none.

In Peace, Love, and Joy

People of this world
Judge themselves and others
By what they do.
The list is endless.
What kind of work?
How much are they worth?
Where do they live?
What kind of education?
How much power do they have?
Do they write, draw, compose?
There are a thousand criteria
Used to judge the self.
None of these is relevant
To our true identity.
Where are peace and joy?

Since we are only love,
Everything we do
Can be done with love.
Anything done with love
Places it beyond judgment.
It shines with
Divine radiance.
There is no criterion
For judging any act of love.
Every act of love merely is.
Everything done with love
Is in harmony with God's Will.
In that harmony,
Is the peace and joy,
Where the Self rests secure.

Unforgiving

Judged a failure by himself,
Although others might not agree.
He felt that way right to the end.
"At least in dying, let me prove my worth," he said.

Both sad and exalted, this view of self,
Feeling the pain of failure,
Yet to the end, unwilling to give up,
In facing death, demonstrating his worth.

How are we to judge a man?
By what he achieves or by what he believes?
Can one judge not knowing life's plan?
Condemnation all too readily at hand.

Affluence

Will I ever be affluent
No matter how much money I have?
The depression, you see, penetrated me
And caused the mind to believe
In fear and scarcity.
Can one escape their time and place
To fully embrace God's limitless Grace
And know only the power of Being?

For others, it's a race
That generates hate.
Religion for some
Restricts their view.
Experience distorts the mind,
So it does not easily find
Its way to another's heart.
Remove the memory of time and place
To let the Self be revealed.
No easy task to undo the past,
To unmask the Eternal that resides in all.
Love's affluence knows no limit.
But one must believe in its power.
There is no scarcity except in the mind's eye.

Forgiveness, not Vengeance

"'Vengeance is mine,' sayeth the Lord."
Conjures up images of the God,
Of "The Battle Hymn of the Republic,"
Or "Onward Christian Soldiers."

"'Vengeance is mine,' sayeth the Lord."
Is best understood as a projection
Of man's own vengefulness
To avoid responsibility for it.

Better, "'Forgiveness is thine,' sayeth the Lord."
Conjuring up images of God
As love, benevolence, and empowerment.
As from the Golden Rule, love others as yourself.

God has nothing to forgive.
Only we need forgiveness
For our misperceptions.
Forgiveness is the pathway of Love.

Forgiveness Is the Key

Forgiveness is the key
That heals the fear in me.
Attacks that seem to come from others
Are actualy only fears that the ego mothers.
Knowing that thoughts of attack are mine
Heals the fear of others in my mind.

Forgiveness is the key
That ends all judgment by me.
If I project my fears onto others,
I judge with fear and hatred
Instead of the forgiveness that
Replaces judging with loving.

Forgiveness is the key
That no harm is meant for me.
It is only my perception that
From God's love, there are exemptions.
Through forgiveness I learn and teach
Love's universe has no exception.

Forgiveness is the key
That unlocks the love that's me.
Only through forgiving all
Does fear and hatred finally fall,
Leaving only love to give,
With only joy to live.

The Spiritual Fire

At first just a flicker,
As the measuring sticks of judgment
Fuel the fire of enlightenment.
The fire burns brightly,
As the judging self is consumed.
In the secure warmth of ego embers glow
Comes the knowing of joy and peace.

Power, Unity, Love

Power to the people is a political statement
Of profound spiritual truth.
Consciousness, the soul, is the collective source
Of all cultural creation.
People are the source of that power
Through shared beliefs and collective consent.
Power is delegated to their political leaders.
Underlying this delegation are two unchanging facts:

Creation is a seamless Oneness.
Leaders who ignore, forget, or don't realize
This basic reality lose their empowerment.
Cultures that attempt to violate this basic unity
Are destined to destructive diversity.
E Pluribus Unum, the many are one.

One of Many

Religion seems to separate
Muslim, Christian, Jew,
Hindu, Buddhist, Sikh,
To name a few.
Within each religion,
Endless denominations
Further divide.
But creation is
One seamless whole.
Yet, man divides creation
Into bits and pieces.
Determined to disbelieve
In its unity.
No part is more right
Or better than another.

There is but a single belief:
GOD AND MAN ARE ONE.
Creation has no exceptions.
No one is left out or behind,
Belief in separateness
Breeds superiority,
Confusing the human mind.
Behind this illusion,
God's Love binds all humankind.
Love's destiny made manifest
In every single one of us.
Love's universality sets us free
To recognize the Divine State
That all with God create.

Religions and the Religious

Belief is a blinder to religious truth,
A limitation to our openness with Creation.
If you think you know,
You are no longer open to the Great Mystery.

Truth is divided into the known, the unknown, and the unknowable.
The unknowable is the subject of religion;
The known and the unknown the subject of science.
Any religion that claims the known is not religious.

Religions that claim the truth divide.
Truth cannot be discovered by others for you.
Religious truth is a self-engaging experience,
Exploring the connection of self with Creation

Following a Christ, Mohammed, or Buddha
Will not make you into one.
Their followers divide humanity
By their divergent beliefs of superiority.

The unity of their founder's original truth
Must be rediscovered through each individual's experience.
No one else can tell you what to believe.
Don't become separated from Creation's Oneness.

The Three that Are One

The three religions of the "Book,"
In conflict so often over the years,
All proclaim there is but one God.
Could not this One be the same
For Muslim, Christian, and Jew?
The mystic say "S/He" is the same,
And inward dwells among all three,
Along with all humanity.

Our separateness seems so manifest,
Confirmed in conflict's spotlighted glare.
The healing oneness overlooked
By prejudice, ignorance, and fear.
What does it take to heal the gulf
That cultural differences make?
Can it be done by quiet ones
Who know the Peace and Joy within?

A Thanksgiving Day Prayer

Our Father is always with us,
A seamless Unity of Spirit,
A oneness of Love.
But we of misplaced faith
See ourselves as frail and weak,
Vulnerable to death's
Every beck and call,
Knowing the fear of separation.

Awake to know your Loving Self!
Find the Face of God in all our hearts.
God is Love; there is no other.
Live life to reveal Love's truth.
Let Love heal the separation.
Be home in Love's brilliant light
That casts no shadow anywhere.
God is Love, and so are we.

Saint Francis of Assisi at Christmas

The popularity and wealth of a rich merchant's son,
The power and prestige of a warrior knight,
All that the external world of his time offered,
St. Francis rejected and chose instead a Spiritual path.
He knew the Self would not be found in the material world;
Only in Universal Love could his spirit be discovered.
Our time, like his, offers external rewards
That mislead and confound the ego self.
Only when we manifest Unconditional Love
Will the true Self be revealed.

The star of Christmas, symbol of Eternal Love's light,
Find it, Close your eyes, sit in the silence, know your source.
In the material pageantry that Christmas has become,
Will the spiritual self be found hidden within these false dreams?
Let the love behind the gifts shine through,
Let the affection of family and friends light the way.
Let the holiday's abundance remind us there is no scarcity.
Unconditional love knows no limits in time or space.
Be a St. Francis. Be your true Self this Christmas.

The Christmas Promise

Love's light shines every Christmastime
To pierce the heart's darkest gloom.
From soul to soul in every man
It spans the globe in every land.

Encircled by a ring of light,
The world, transformed, this holy night.
As though walking hand in hand,
All understand the common bond of man.

No longer separate and apart,
United by love's healing grace.
One world, one God, one race.
Peace, God's gift from the start.

The Christmas Holidays

The shortening days' decreasing light
    is heightened as snow clouds sail into sight.
The evening air is still and crisp,
    and frost has darkened each rosebud's tip.
But hark! Across winter's darkening gloom,
    a carol shatters the icy tomb.
A red, enshrouded, rotund form
    of fun and laughter performs.
In contrast with white, glistening snow
    are holly balsam and mistletoe.

The birth of a babe to man is known,
    the light of love in life is shown.
As surely as the light of spring
    is born in winter's dark sheltering,
So love, as the seed of life,
    blossoms in a garden of peril and strife.
Let carols be sung and trees lighted,
    feasts be spread and poems recited.
For only in the festivals of man
    is the hope sustained that ages span.

Christmas

A babe is born, all hope renewed,
A world redeemed by love revealed.
The manger scene, this world renounced,
His power from a greater Source.
A universe of love transcends
Time and place to speak to us
Of our eternal home.
Entry is gained by giving love instead of hate,
An end to pain and fear, death and sin,
Alive instead, within Love's embrace.
Forever One, eternally joined in Peace and Joy.
It all begins that Christmas night,
When Love explodes in brilliant light.
The darkness now forever gone,
For light once seen remains within.

The Climb

Life's trail starts in a watery marsh of rising mist,
Wanders through fields of flowers and sunlit song,
Into a cool, shaded wood, stretching up the hill,
Rising beyond necessity's constricted view
Onto a cloud enshrouded upper path,
Breaking free into vastness hardly grasped.

The Courage to Be

Each individual a separate spark of consciousness,
Yet part of the total light of humanity.
In sharing each individual awareness,
The collective experience of humanity
Expands, benefiting all by adding to the light.
It takes courage to be open and honest,
But this is the only way humanity
Moves toward its ultimate destiny
Of universal enlightenment.
Have the courage to be!

Eternal I

At
The start
I was there.
Infancy, childhood, youth, too,
Adulthood's long stretch of years,
College, job, family, friends, illness, health.
Detached observer, never changing.
Growing, aging, coming, going,
Ever present Now.
Ever I
AM.

Life and Death

There are no two opposites
more strongly believed in
than the dualities of life and death.
What if life and death are actually the same?
Death merely a signpost on life's endless road,
just as birth is a signpost at the other end.
What we call life merely physical existence
between birth and death.
Death merely marking a transition
to another form of existence, rather than life's end.
The perceptual shift necessary,
stresses the rational mind rooted in materialism.
To question the basic duality of life and death
opens the mind to myriad new ideas,
re-creating the world in which we live.

Light

Life is like a burning candle,
Radiating light and warmth into the darkness,
Bathing all in its radiance,
While the candle continuously shrinks
Into its finite, inevitable end.

When the light flickers out,
All that is left is a blackened wick
And a pool of melted wax.
The physical remains
Of the light's former source.

Where has the light gone?
Traveling through infinite space
To an unknown destination
Beyond imagining, soon to be
Renewed by yet another candle.

The Doorway

Grieve not for the body's demise,
Celebrate spirit's passage to a new sunrise.
Physically no longer here,
Released instead among the so-called dead.

Remember the warmth of love still glows
Within those whose infinite spirit grows
Beyond temporal time and place,
Together in God's Creation forever.

So many have gone before,
Yet this passage so many still abhor,
Death seen only as end, rather than beginning.
Farewell spirit pioneer, the new adventure draws near.

Fear not, because love abides on both sides.
Death's abyss only divides
The body from where pure spirit presides.
Rejoice in death's release, where all find peace.

Life's long learning, a travail of spiritual yearning,
Making ready for the soul's journey of emancipation.
Free of all physical constraint, no pain or complaint,
Bathed in light, all doubt absolved, true knowing regained.

The Eve of a New Millennium

Two thousand years of war and strife,
The lesson taught but still unlearned.
How often will it repeat?
How much longer will it take?
Fears of loss, scarcity, and death
Take control of our lives.
Brotherhood lost in rivalry and competition.
Winning and losing the game of life.
The unlearned lesson so simple
Yet so hard to grasp.
All worldly experiences
Seem to contradict.
How could it be right?
At some level of being
The truth is known.
Love, abundance, and brotherhood
The foundation of eternal creation.
Know this truth.
It will set us free
In the Peace and Joy
We were born to be.

The Quark

Psychology was shaped by biology and physics.
Now the ways are parting.
Psychology and biology left behind
In the material world,
While physics explores the quark.

A quark is what remains
After the tiniest particle of matter disappears.
Matter seems to be ephemeral.
The Universe is found to rest
On a whole lot less than physicists expected.

Psychology persists in believing
The brain creates the mind.
When the brain dies, the mind is gone.
But what of the ephemeral bit: consciousness?
Is it the quark of the mind?

Is consciousness more basic
Than either brain or mind?
Hinduism, Buddhism, and mysticism
All express this idea in similar yet different forms.
Where now is the difference between science and religion?

The Truth We Deny

Hostility begets hostility,
Aggression generates fear,
Fear creates separation,
Separation permits projection of hate,
Hate justifies anger,
Anger generates hostility,
War often the result.
Today's war sows the seeds
Of tomorrow's hatred and hostility.

Peace is not attained by war.
Peace is Love, and Love is Peace.
Love and Peace create Oneness.
In Oneness, there is no separation.
No other to hate and fight.
Such is the unity of Love.
In Love's Power lies everlasting Peace.
Can we believe this Truth?
Can we live Love and break the cycle of hate?

The Twentieth Century

The twentieth century, one hundred years of a world at war,
From the sinking of the *Maine* that presaged the age,
To WW One and Two, Vietnam, Lebanon, Iraq, Iran, Afghanistan.
Testimony to belief in the idea that might makes right,
That imposed authority can command the mind of man.

The allies of one war the enemies of the next.
Truth the captive of conflicting propaganda,
Always a new belief to justify the slaughter.
Fascism, Communism, Capitalism, Buddhist, Christian, Muslim, Jew,
Attempted domination by a zealot self-righteous few.

Thoughts placed into man's mind by men,
Choices we ourselves commend, creating a hell we did not intend.
Turk, Armenian, Iraqi, Kurd, Native, Immigrant,
Atheist, Evangelist, White, Black, rejected other.
How long can man continue not to understand?

The consequence of attack is fear, hate, and dreams of revenge,
They start the vicious cycle of hostility all over again,
Escalating to the ultimate fear of nuclear holocaust,
Aggression taken to the point of inconceivable loss,
Inhumanity enthroned without pity or remorse.

A century that denies that within the minds of all
Is a consciousness beyond extinction, above war's pall,
Seeking the self-respect that tolerance generates,
Yearning to unite within love's encircling ring,
Realizing the soul fulfillment brotherhood brings.

Can the twenty-first century be the age of universal love,
An age where the haves no longer disdain countless others,
Creating dignity for all by recognizing everyone's worth,
Realizing love of self and others can never be independent,
Making the planet safe, not exporting hate into outer space?

Think Again

Is this the year?
Oh please say it's so!
Haven't we waited
Long enough
To reach the turning point
Of no return?
Gone forever, belief in
Scarcity, separation, despair,
Fear, hate, revenge,
Discrimination, inequality.
The end of war.

Replaced with universal
Love, Peace, Joy,
Oneness of Spirit,
Bountiful creativity,
Limitless opportunity.
Only belief
Need change.
Is this the year
The critical mass
Is reached,
The new course set?

Time

There is only one time,
And it is now.
There is no yesterday,
Nor tomorrow.
Now is the only time there is.

We seem to exist
In three time frames:
Yesterday, today, and tomorrow.
A fantasy of the ego,
For now is all there is.

Eternity is the only reality.
An unbroken time dimension
Of past, present, and future,
Extending infinitely
In the spiritual dimension.

In it all are united with all.
There can be no separation
Without time's existence.
Distance requires time,
Separation requires distance.

The illusion of the ego
As a separate entity
Demands the existence
Of serial time
To maintain the delusion.

Unconditional Love

Love is the one thing you cannot give away.
Its power is enhanced by giving.
It returns in unexpected ways.
Some who fear its awesome power
May respond with hostility and anger.
The self-sacrifice that resulted
In the crucifixion of Jesus
Created the world's greatest love symbol.
God's unconditional love will be
Manifested in this world.
Be its instrument.
You are the one.

Unintended Consequences

Mystics say everything is already perfect.
A Course in Miracles says there are no accidents.
How, then, can there be unintended consequences?
Maybe there aren't any; we only think there are.
Imperfect perception leads to faulty predictions.
Faulty predictions open the door to unintended consequences.
For the enlightened seer, there are no unintended consequences
Because s/he is totally aware, in a state of total Being.
Unintended consequences result from faulty thinking.
There is no fault in being, only in mind.
In the separate ego state, unintended consequences abound,
Some are thought to be "good," others "bad."
But in reality, they are only thought projections of intellect.

What Is Life?

Life in this world is both physical and spiritual,
Just as light is both particle and wave.
If you look one way, you see only photons.
If you look another way, you see only waves.
Life as seen by science is physical.
Life as seen by religion is spiritual.
In this world, the physical masks the spiritual,
And the spiritual is not easily known.
When death transforms life,
The physical disappears,
And the spiritual is revealed.
What good then is knowing
Only of the physical?
Know, then, the unity that is life.

Whose Plan?

Dinosaurs, inhabitants for sixty million years,
Dead because of cataclysmic force.
Ice ages replaced by warmer climes.
Continents float on molten rock,
Drift together, collide, then part.
Mountains form, erode away.
Seas rise then recede.
Species appear then become extinct.
Change is the only changeless force.
Man insecurely rests within Earth's evolution,
Part of a cosmos so vast, so grand,
Exceeding human comprehension.
Who knows Creation's Master Plan?

Words

Words are culture-bound
Vehicles for the communication
Of thoughts and feelings
From one mind to another.
Always inadequate projections
Of personal meaning and interpretation,
Despite attempts to be objective.
There is greater agreement and understanding
For external events than for inner states,
Intracultural distortion less than intercultural,
Historical communication, bridging time, even more limited.
How inadequately words communicate feelings and emotions,
Spiritual transformation, or enlightenment.
The Tower of Babel symbolizes not only language differences,
But it also represents our inability to bridge the mind gap of our separated state,
The inadequacy of words to communicate the Oneness of our Being.

Awaken

Life has no opposite.
Yet we think it does.
We call it death.

God is eternal.
Due to our unity,
So are we.

God and we are one.
God is everlasting.
So are we.

Fear is thinking
We are separate
From God.

Belief in separation
Makes death seem possible,
Making fear real.

Ever Am, Ever Am.
Awaken to the light
Of the true self.

Live the life
Of our true identity.
Go in Peace, Joy, and Love.

The Message of Easter

From the cross, He gives the world forgiveness.
"Forgive them Father, for they know not what they do."
In forgiving another, one's self is forgiven.
The anger of perceived attack and difference replaced
With love, in the realization that all are one in God.

From the cross, He demonstrates to the world God's judgment.
He offers the Kingdom of Heaven to a thief and murderer.
Judged by the world as the most unworthy,
Not judged, only loved by God, as are we all.
God judges no one; only we judge others and ourselves.

From the cross, He renounces fear in the world.
The world offers no suffering worse than crucifixion,
Prolonged agony, and eventual death.
But Spirit is neither harmed nor destroyed.
Since you are not a body, no real harm can come to you.

From the tomb, He demonstrates to the world true reality.
His resurrection shows He is spirit that survives bodily death.
Death and suffering are only of the flesh.
Death is the ultimate separation, if we think we are only a body.
But there is no death, only spiritual at-one-ment of man and God.

The message of Easter is heal the separation of man from God.
By forgiveness, we move from the aloneness that generates fear and
Anger to the unity that is love.
By nonjudgment, we move from rejecting others to the loving
Realization of others as self.
By releasing ourselves from the fear of death,

We come to realize our true at-one-ment with All.
We are, as only a loving God could create us, invulnerable
And secure in a spiritual world of love, at peace.
Seek not for security in the material world, for you will not find it there.
Find it instead within your mind, where Love always resides.
Go forth into the world, radiating the Peace that comes from
Knowing there is nothing to fear.
You will be the light of the world's everlasting springtime.

You Are the Plan

In life, there are no accidents,
Nothing by chance,
Everything a purpose
In fulfilling the Divine Plan.

How then do we account
For bad and evil events,
Sickness and death,
Pain and suffering?

Are all bad things
Illusions of our collective nightmare,
Creations of the human mind
Apart from the Divine?

Are we free to choose
Between heaven and hell,
Creating a reality
That reflects that choice?

Will all suffering
Cause us to choose again,
Choosing love instead of fear,
Unity instead of separation?

Man as participant in creation
Fulfills God's will
Freedom and action,
Complete the Divine Plan.

Know your Divine potential,
Create the unity of love,
Know its joy and peace,
Experience your limitless self.

Creation's Power

Victor Hugo said:
"There is nothing so powerful as an idea whose time has come."
I say, "There is nothing so powerful as human thought."
By perception and projection, it creates the world as we know it.
This shared creation we call life.
Its time is always, its power is infinite, its reality is the All.
Create only what you wish in fulfillment of your highest self.
It is your greatest gift, your Divine destiny, the ideal world.
Love manifest is creation's power.
Go forth in love, peace, and joy.

A Course in Miracles—Conversation with God Prayer

Our Father is always with us;
We are one in Creation,
A seamless unity of Spirit.
Love is the only truth.
Let us go forth in love
And find the face of God
In all our hearts.
Let life reveal the truth:
God is love, and so are we.
There is no other.
What is done to one
Is done to all.
Life without end. Amen.